Praise for Carmen Renee

Berry presents a refreshing, innovative, and clear historical perspective of a biblical/scriptural view of sexuality. She deals with nonnegotiable core beliefs while embracing a diversity of convictions among those who are followers of Jesus Christ. We found her writing to be thoughtful, provocative, challenging, yet full of grace and delightfully expressed.

—Clifford and Joyce Penner, authors of *The Gift of Sex*

Carmen Berry has done a great job again. *The Unauthorized Guide to Sex and the Church* builds excellent bridges between biblical truths and sexuality and is a great, balanced resource on sexuality in the life of the church. As a minister and psychologist who specializes in sex therapy, I shall recommend this book to patients who find it helpful to be grounded in the understanding of the relationship between their faith and human sexuality. The humor, while relaying an enormous amount of data, makes the book very readable.

—Ralph H. Earle, Ph.D., A.B.P.P., President,
Psychological Counseling Services, Ltd.

The Unauthorized Guide to
Sex and the Church

CARMEN RENEE BERRY

W PUBLISHING GROUP
A Division of Thomas Nelson Publishers
Since 1798

www.wpublishinggroup.com

Published by W Publishing Group, a Division of Thomas Nelson, Inc., P.O. Box 141000, Nashville, Tennessee
37214.

W Publishing Group books may be purchased in bulk for educational, business, fund-raising, or sales pro-
motional use. For information, please e-mail SpecialMarkets@ThomasNelson.com.

All Scripture quotations, unless otherwise indicated, are taken from The Holy Bible, New International
Version (NIV). Copyright © 1973, 1978, 1984, International Bible Society. Used by permission of Zondervan
Bible Publishers.

Other Scripture references are from the following sources:

The King James Version of the Bible (KJV).

The Holy Bible, Today's New International® Version (TNIV©). Copyright 2001, 2005 by International Bible
Society®. Used by permission of International Bible Society®. All rights reserved worldwide. "TNIV" and
"Today's New International Version" are trademarks registered in the United States Patent and Trademark
Office by International Bible Society®.

Editorial Staff: Deborah Wiseman, Todd Kinde, Bethany Bothman, Laura Weller, Rhonda Hogan,
    Renee Chavez
Page Design: Lori Lynch, Book and Graphic Design, Nashville, TN

Library of Congress Cataloging-in-Publication Data

Berry, Carmen Renee.
  The unauthorized guide to sex and the church / by Carmen Berry.
      p. cm.
  Includes index.
  ISBN 0-8499-4544-5
  1. Sex—Religious aspects—Christianity. I. Title.
  BT708.B47 2005
  241'.66—dc22   2004029445

Printed in the United States of America
05 06 07 08 09 RRD 9 8 7 6 5 4 3 2 1

Dedicated to my mother, Mary Ellen Berry,
because every time she tells her friend
I dedicated this book to her, she'll have
to say the word "sex."

Contents

Introduction

What Does Jesus Mean to My Sex Life?

Sex is not a prevalent topic of conversation at most churches—at least not when it comes to personal disclosure. Let's face it: sex scares a lot of Christians. Some Christians are afraid of being ridiculed or shamed if they are honest about their sexual needs, desires, or activities. Many don't want to discuss sexual issues for fear of getting tangled up in sexual misunderstandings. Others are resistant to entertaining differing ideas about sexuality because they fear that somewhere along the way without meaning to, they will compromise their faith. Sex can be a very scary topic for many Christians who struggle with personal sexuality in isolated silence.

At the same time it can seem that sex is all the church talks about. Spokespeople who identify themselves as Christians go on television animatedly discussing sexually related issues such as homosexuality, abortion, or in vitro fertilization. Passionate declarations are made about the merits of school-based sex education, teenage pregnancies, condom distribution, and sexually transmitted diseases. Christians never seem to lack strong opinions when it comes to sex, and in today's political climate, we are often outspoken and seemingly quite sure of our positions.

Unfortunately, sexual issues are not as clear cut as some Christian groups make them appear. It is commonly misconstrued that Judeo-Christian sexual morality is a concrete, set-in-stone code of conduct upon which all Jews and Christians throughout history have agreed—a misconception most often promoted by Christians themselves. An honest look at history reveals that what we have considered acceptable sexual morality and practice for the past two thousand years, and even back to the origins of Old Testament Law, has been defined and redefined repeatedly. Too often the church has created a climate in which sexual proclamations are plentiful, but safe places to discuss personal sexuality are scarce. This damages Christians in at least three ways:

1. We Stop Listening to Each Other

Whenever I believe I am right (and everyone else is wrong), I tell anyone within earshot what I think and I stop listening. And why should I listen when I already know I'm right? My goal is to educate others in the truth, right?

Similarly, when churches and individual Christians are certain they know what's right, they do all the talking and stop listening. Declarations abound. Conversation ceases. Lines are drawn and the church is divided.

Our convictions, based on our interpretations of Scripture or church tradition, can carry the additional weight of being "God's will." Whenever people are certain they are speaking for God, I, for one, assume they aren't. I believe a spiritually mature Christian is one who is cautious about putting words into

God's mouth. Nevertheless, numerous Christian groups and individuals regularly make this claim. For example, there are those among us who insist that, if you're a real Christian, you will be pro-life, antihomosexual, and always vote Republican. Other Christians are equally insistent about their pro-choice and pro-gay positions, calling for other believers to hold a Democratic or Independent voting record. Conversations between these two factions are rare.

> Our sexuality, as God created it, can be likened to a multi-faceted diamond, its light reaching out in many directions and its center reflecting the intimacy which is at the very heart of God.[1]
> —MARGARET GILL

I do believe that there are universal truths, most significantly, the love of God as expressed through Christ. But when we lack humility and openness to the leading of God's Spirit, we stop listening to each other. A closed mind and arrogant heart are never biblical.

2. We Damage the Church's Credibility

In addition to the damage caused within the church, the church loses credibility in society when we do not acknowledge the diverse opinions held by fellow believers. We undermine what moral authority the church could potentially command when we appear surprised, perturbed, or dismissive of other believers in the face of disagreement. Nonbelievers see disrespect among believers and a divided church, no matter how much we may pretend we're "united in Christ."

3. We Lose Our Personal Sense of Sexual Morality

Here's a game: I'll say a word, and you respond with the first thing that comes to your mind. Okay, the first word is *priest*.

What came to your mind?

If it was *child molester,* you're not alone.

Now for the second word—*evangelist.*

You'd be right on target if you associated it with *soliciting prostitutes* or *extramarital affairs.*

Christians aren't doing so well in the practice-what-we-preach department. The misconduct among our ranks is judged appalling by anyone's standards, Christian or otherwise. Sexual scandals of monumental proportions are perpetrated by clergy and laity. Check out these statistics:

- It's hard to estimate how many children were abused by Catholic priests in recent years. In California alone, close to eight hundred claims accusing two hundred priests were filed before December 31, 2003. Based on an amalgamation of sources, as many as three thousand priests (2 percent of Catholic clergy) abused children over the past fifty years. Thomas Plante, professor of psychology at Santa Clara University, estimates that these priests abused approximately 24,000 victims.[2]

- Of three hundred Protestant clergy surveyed by Richard Blackmon, 38 percent admitted to inappropriate sexual contact with parishioners; 12 percent admitted to sexual intercourse.[3]

- The divorce rate among the general population is 35 percent. Divorce among Christians? It's also 35 percent. According to a study released in 2004 by the Barna Research Group, Christians are just as likely to divorce as nonbelievers. No difference at all.[4]

- No one knows for sure how many Christians are into Internet pornography, but researchers are trying to make estimates. In August 2000,

Christianity Today reported that 36 percent of the laity and 33 percent of the clergy they surveyed had visited sexually explicit Web sites. More than half (53 percent) of the clergy visited these sites more than once.

- Another survey sponsored by the Fuller Institute of Church Growth in 1991 revealed that 37 percent of the pastors surveyed confessed to having been involved in "inappropriate sexual behavior with someone in the church."[5]

WHAT DOES JESUS MEAN TO MY SEX LIFE?

Christian is a term that can be used as a religious word or a political word, a slur or an honor. It's a loosey-goosey sort of word that has been spiritualized, politicized, and even demonized. I don't expect everyone who reads this book to agree with my definition. But for clarity, I'll define the term as I understand it. A Christian is a person who believes that God loves him or her so much that God took on human form in Jesus—who was simultaneously fully human and fully divine. Through Jesus's birth, life, death, and resurrection, a personal relationship with God was made possible.

> A Christian is a person who believes that God loves him or her so much that God took on human form in Jesus—who was simultaneously fully human and fully divine.

We don't have to agree on sex to be Christians—we just need to agree on Christ.

I believe an unbroken chain of believers has embraced this perspective, starting from the first Christians through today. This belief is best summarized in the Nicene creed, a statement created in the year AD 325, which most

Christian denominations—conservative, mainline, and liberal—still affirm today. The gist of the Nicene creed is the assertion that God is composed of three persons: God the Father, God the Son, and God the Holy Spirit. Most significant to me is the person of Jesus as fully human and fully divine—a mystery none of us will ever fully grasp but can accept by faith.

I'm not trying to convince anyone about the person of Jesus or the core message of the gospel. Theologically conservative Christians generally accept the divinity-humanity of Jesus, as do I, consequently. That's another conversation for another book. Rather, Jesus is my entry point into this discussion. The fact of Jesus isn't up for debate. It's a given.

 The Nicene Creed

We believe in one God the Father Almighty, Maker of heaven and earth, and of all things visible and invisible.

And in one Lord Jesus Christ, the only-begotten Son of God, begotten of the Father before all worlds, God of God, Light of Light, Very God of Very God, begotten, not made, being of one substance with the Father by whom all things were made; who for us men, and for our salvation, came down from heaven, and was incarnate by the Holy Spirit of the Virgin Mary, and was made man, and was crucified also for us under Pontius Pilate. He suffered and was buried, and the third day he rose again according to the Scriptures, and ascended into heaven, and sitteth on the

> > >

> > >

right hand of the Father. And he shall come again with glory to judge both the quick and the dead, whose kingdom shall have no end.

And we believe in the Holy Spirit, the Lord and Giver of Life, who proceedeth from the Father and the Son, who with the Father and the Son together is worshipped and glorified, who spoke by the prophets. And we believe in one holy catholic and apostolic Church. We acknowledge one baptism for the remission of sins. And we look for the resurrection of the dead, and the life of the world to come. Amen.

But how we interpret and apply Jesus's teachings to our lives is very much up for debate. Christians have struggled with this from the git-go, saying, "Well, being a Christian means this . . ." While others said, "No, that's not right. Knowing Jesus means that . . ." The first believers tried to answer this question. The apostles tried to answer this question. The church fathers debated and wrote and debated some more. Groups were formed; battle lines were drawn. Literally. During the past two thousand years, Christians have killed one another in defense of their interpretation of the person of Jesus. How utterly ironic and horrifying. The church should be ashamed of the infighting, the hostility, the bloodshed, the sorrow—the sheer number of denominations—generated over the years due to theological and political differences.

As the following historical overview will show, from time to time Christians have gotten *the gospel* confused with their *interpretation* and *application of* the gospel. The gospel and its interpretation aren't one and the same—

one is a nonnegotiable historical and spiritual truth about the immense love of God and specifically about the profound person of Christ. The other . . . isn't.

Too often, Christians discuss sexuality as if holding certain beliefs or supporting specific sexual behaviors were synonymous with being a Christian. Please let me emphasize that a person's salvation is based only on faith in Jesus Christ. Period. God's love for you is not based on who you do or do not fantasize about, whether or not you masturbate, who you do or do not have sex with, whether or not you've had an abortion, whether or not you've had an affair, or if you've been paid for sexual favors. You are not more loved by God if you're straight and loathed if you're gay; not more loved if you've been faithful to your spouse and loathed if you haven't; not more loved if you live a sexless life.

When we properly separate the gospel from its human interpretation, God is glorified and people are transformed. When we get the two confused and promote our application *as if it were* the gospel, we can become the most judgmental, hostile, and offensive people on the planet. We repel people from God when we arrogantly believe our theological systems are synonymous with truth. We deteriorate into hateful creatures while insisting we fully understand Jesus as God's expression of infinite, inclusive love.

→ Eastern Orthodoxy on Church Rules

Finally, it must not be forgotten that the Church is not to be identified with her rules. The Church indeed has rules, but she has much else besides. She has within her

> > >

> > >

treasures of another order and another value besides her canons. She has her theology, her spirituality, her mysticism, her liturgy, her morality. And it is most important not to confuse the Gospel and the Pedalion (a collection of canons), theology and legislation, morality and jurisprudence. Each is on a different level and to identify them completely would be to fall into a kind of heresy. The canons are at the service of the Church; their function is to guide her members on the way to salvation and to make following that way easier.[6]

My goal in writing this book is twofold. First, I want to help individual Christians make informed choices about their personal beliefs regarding sexuality. As adult Christians who are responsible for our personal relationships with God, we need to decide for ourselves what we believe rather than leaving these important issues up to our pastors, families, or even peers. I hope this book helps you to deepen your faith and encounter God at a more personal level through struggling with issues of sexuality. There are few, if any, areas of life that sex does not influence, from the very private and personal to the very public and political arenas.

Second, I hope to encourage Christians to talk much more respectfully among ourselves about sexual concerns. Some Christians have become so insulated from the rest of the church that we don't recognize that differences of opinion exist among believers. Examples used in this book will illustrate that Christians can hold firm to an orthodox faith in Christ and simultaneously embrace views of sexuality that differ. These opinions can even be diametrically opposed. A particular congregation or denomination may teach that there is only one acceptable interpretation of sexual morality and practice, but neither an open look at history nor the current assessment of today's church support this opinion.

Sexual beliefs vary from Christian to Christian, denomination to denomination—and yet we all remain parts of the same universal church. We are all members of the same body of Christ. I pray that we discover our common love of Christ is stronger than our disagreements over sex.

Who we are in Christ should and will make a difference to our sexual lives as the Holy Spirit continues to love us. How we apply the gospel to our lives is our spiritual work, as the Holy Spirit transforms us into the image of Christ. Our responsibility as maturing Christians is to learn, to think, to ponder, to pray, to ask, to recommend, to share, to rethink, and to allow the Holy Spirit to change us into more exact likenesses of Christ through the process of learning, thinking, pondering, praying, asking, recommending, rethinking, and sharing. I believe the Holy Spirit teaches the heart that is asking questions, longing to love in a more vulnerable way—not those who think they have all the answers and are closed up tight. The possible answers to the question, "What does Jesus mean to my life?" and more specifically, "What does Jesus mean to my sex life?" may be more varied than you think.

PART 1

Property, Purity, and Practices

Sex itself can be a passionate, even irrational, experience. So can trying to discuss it. The topic does not lend itself to tidy categories that are easily explored in a logical manner. At the risk of having some elements of sexuality refusing to fit nicely into my schema, I've divided the topic into three larger themes: (1) sexual issues related to property rights and body ownership, (2) sexual purity, and (3) sexual practices. These themes are based on the Jewish mind-set as described in the Old Testament. While we may not immediately place sexual issues in these same categories today, Western thought still reflects its basis in Judeo-Christian ideas. Making these categories more conscious, I believe, can help us as both individual Christians and the church at large to better conceptualize, express, and understand divergent opinions regarding sex.

PROPERTY RIGHTS AND
BODY OWNERSHIP

Who owns what, or even who owns whom, has always been a concern of human beings. Rights to ownership define how we perceive ourselves, our place in society, and the manner in which we relate to one another. Obviously, those who get to do the owning have more power over those who are limited in their ownership. A significant concern for our lives today is who owns us. To what extent do we own our own bodies, and what choices are we allowed to make about our personal sexuality?

Viewing our bodies as property may seem a bit archaic, even irrelevant, yet this concept is quite vital and volatile in the church today. For example, one of the major dividing issues in the church is abortion. All arguments boil down to the question of body ownership. Pro-life advocates engage in the body-ownership debate by claiming that "abortion is a violation of the rights of the human fetus." The mother may have ownership of her body, but she does not have ownership of her baby's body. Pro-lifers believe that life begins at conception and that each life owns its own body.[1] Pro-choice proponents insist that life does not begin at conception. It is therefore argued that a woman has the right to decide what happens to her own body. Her property rights must not be limited by giving unmerited status to a "fetus." We'll be talking more about abortion and other body-ownership issues facing us today later in the book.

SEXUAL PURITY

A friend of mine, who is an excellent preacher, recently spoke on Christian sexuality. He said, "I was taught two contradictory things about sex. First, it's dirty. Second, I should save it for the one I love." No clearer statement could be made about the dichotomy presented to today's Christians. We are encouraged to remain chaste until we marry and then share this beautiful experience with our forever-spouse. In the meantime, don't touch, don't look, don't ask, don't explore. Sex is dirty, and it will make you dirty too.

Where did we get the idea that our bodies—and more specifically our sexuality—are unclean, perhaps even evil? With little clarity, we are often taught a mishmash of dismal decrees on our physical selves: that our "flesh" leads us away from God, and yet Jesus became "flesh" and dwelt among us; that our bodies are separate from our spirits, and yet, as orthodox believers, we hold tenaciously to the bodily resurrection of Jesus; the less sexual we are, the more spiritual we are, and yet God created both male and female with the declaration that it wasn't good for us to be alone. Contradictions abound in Christian thinking. And we, as individuals trying to live our lives as God would desire, are flipped and flopped as these ideas collide. So what's the bottom line? Are our bodies temples of God or the source of all that is vile and evil in this world? Is sex a beautiful expression of our love or something dirty to be feared?

SEXUAL PRACTICES

Theological beliefs impact not only how we view sex as a whole, but specific sexual activities as well. Do you believe there are sexual activities that are forbidden for all people in any context? Or do you believe that between married, consenting adults, what they do in their bedrooms is their prerogative? How do you view such sexual activities as masturbation or oral sex? There is not a consensus on which sexual practices are acceptable and which are not. This is often rooted in our differences in the interpretation of Scripture and what we have been taught by our church tradition. Let's take a look at what Christians have believed over the years, starting with our Jewish beginnings.

Chapter 1

Body Ownership and Dirty Deeds in the Old Testament

An aging nomad named Abraham and Sarah, his postmenopausal wife, were wandering around the desert a few hundred centuries ago. They had lost hope of creating a family. Then God told Abraham he was going to be the father of a huge nation of people. To make a long story short, God did what was promised and gave Abraham and Sarah a son they called Isaac. Isaac became the father of Esau and Jacob. Jacob fathered a number of children; his sons became the sires of the twelve tribes of Israel. Joseph, his most notable son, ended up in Egypt and eventually saved not only his nuclear family from starvation and annihilation but rescued his extended family as well. That was the good news.

The bad news was that the descendants of Abraham were enslaved by the Egyptians and horribly misused. They survived their ordeal by holding together as a family, not as separate individuals who pulled themselves up by their own bootstraps. Survival of an individual outside of a family or tribal unit was impossible in those days. And survival of the family was not guaranteed either. The descendants of Abraham came close to being wiped off the face of the planet more than once. Family became the cornerstone of their culture.

Then Moses came on the scene. He had a few adventures of his own and eventually squared off with Pharaoh, the ruler of Egypt. A few episodes of plagues and pestilence later, the Israelites were released and they took off for the Promised Land. Moses is attributed with writing the first five books of the Bible: Genesis, Exodus, Leviticus, Numbers, and Deuteronomy. While the scholars debate who wrote what, let's assume that Moses was the primary author and look at the guidelines given to the ancient Jews, a set of laws that carefully defined their relationships and behavior. Some related to cleanliness, disease control, and eating practices. Some related to sexual activities. And quite a few related to property rights.

PROPERTY RIGHTS

In our society the individual, rather than the family, is the primary social unit. Individuals may come together to form families, but they remain separate legal entities within that context. It can be hard for us to see life from the standpoint of a collective. But to understand what is taught in the Old Testament, we must recognize that it was written for people who defined themselves by their families.

→ **Song of Songs**

Whenever I've heard a sermon citing the Song of Songs, the preacher has always said that the book described the relationship between Christ and the church. I guess that's one way to avoid the sexual intimacy about which Solomon wrote. Here is a short sampling of how sexuality was celebrated in this Old Testament book:

I belong to my lover,
    and his desire is for me.
Come, my lover, let us go to the countryside,
    let us spend the night in the villages.
Let us go early to the vineyards
    to see if the vines have budded,
    if their blossoms have opened,
    and if the pomegranates are in bloom—
    there I will give you my love.
(Song of Songs 7:10–12 NIV)

THE FAMILY AS PROPERTY

A man's highest calling was to become the patriarch of a family unit. To fulfill this responsibility, the patriarch was given ownership over everyone in his family, as well as over others who served the family, such as slaves and concubines. The man in charge could do pretty much what he liked, although there were some limits set by law meant to protect living property from severe abuse.

Women were forbidden to work outside the home and produce any sort of income. They were valued solely for their ability to procreate. In this ancient society, a woman had little control over whom she married, when she got pregnant, or how many children she would bear. Essentially all females got married upon reaching puberty. There were no other options. This reality is reflected in their language. The Israelites had one word for a woman who had grown to sexual maturity—*ishshah*—that was used interchangeably for woman or wife.[1] If you were an adult woman, you were a wife. To put it in modern terms, men had total control of women and their reproductive rights.

A man could accumulate as many wives as he wanted. Marriages were arranged between families, the father promising to provide a virgin and the future son-in-law to take responsibility for her support. The young teenager would leave her father's home and move into her husband's, although she never became a full member of her husband's family. She was suspended between two households, partly because her tenure as a wife was tenuous. At his discretion, her husband could divorce her. She couldn't divorce him because property can't divorce itself from its master. If her husband divorced her, she would return to her family of origin, if possible, or be out on her own. In either case, she was disgraced in the community.

As the property owner, the groom had the opportunity to take a test drive, so to speak. If, after having sex with his new wife, the husband "disliked her," he was allowed to tell everyone she wasn't a virgin. To defend the family honor against such an accusation, the girl's parents were expected to come up with proof of their daughter's virginity—the sheet from the wedding bed, with blood on it. If proof of virginity could not be produced, the consequences for the young woman were disastrous. She would be dragged through town to the front door of her father's home. There she would be stoned to death, to the horror and disgrace of her parents and extended family. On the other hand, if proof of virginity could be given, the slandering husband would be fined one hundred shekels of silver that would be paid to the girl's father. And in addition, he would never be able to divorce her. Jewish men had the right to divorce their wives simply by handing them written notice. Taking this right away from a man was a big deal.

In addition to wives, men were also allowed to have concubines. The role of the concubine is not clearly defined in the Old Testament. She appears to be a woman with whom a man could have sex and raise a family, but she wasn't a full-fledged wife, and her children were not full-fledged heirs. She had some rights but not as many as the wives and their children were given.

Another member of the Jewish household was the slave. Slaves, with no chance of freedom, were non-Jews who were captured in battle or purchased by the patriarchs. Jewish bondservants were to be given their freedom at some point.

There were some limitations to what a master could do but not enough for me to want to be owned by your average patriarch. For example, if an owner beat his slave to the point that he or she was blinded in one eye or had a tooth knocked out, the slave was to be released "to compensate for" the eye or the tooth (Exod. 21:26–27). Killing one's slave was also not acceptable, but beating one half to death was fine. In Exodus 21:20–21 we read, "Anyone who beats their male or female slave with a rod must be punished if the slave dies as a direct result, but they are not to be punished if the slave recovers after a day or two, since the slave is their property" (TNIV). As long as a slave could recover from the beating, the owner could do as he pleased. The Law read, ". . . since the slave is their property."

Stealing Was Bad

While owning other human beings was allowed, stealing was seriously frowned upon. Survival was as important to the ancient Jews as it is to us. Stealing another man's property decreased rather than increased one's holdings and was seen as a direct threat to the survival of the family. We don't think of stealing in these terms today. No one wants to have a car stolen or his or her house broken into. But a car can be replaced (especially if we have theft insurance). We can equip our homes with stronger security systems and restore our sense of safety. We care more about violations to our persons than to our physical property. But to the ancient Jews, stealing and physical threat were one and the same. Theft of a cow (and all the milk she would produce) could be a horrible loss to a family, a threat to their survival. Their valuables weren't insured and, if destroyed, were gone forever.

Stealing a man's human possessions was considered a real travesty—and this offense was not restricted to literally kidnapping one's slave, wife, or child. Being sexually intimate with another man's human property was also considered stealing. Violating a woman or child sexually was unacceptable, not because of the impact it had on the woman or child, but because it violated the property rights of the man who owned them. Sleeping with another man's wife robbed him of sure knowledge that his children were genuinely his own. And violating the virginity of a young girl decreased her value in the marriage market. The penalties for defiling the property of a father or husband were usually pretty stiff. He may very well be stoned to death. But not always.

If a man had sex with a girl who wasn't engaged, the act was considered to be rape, but the penalty may surprise you. "He shall pay the girl's father fifty shekels of silver. He must marry the girl, for he has violated her. He can never divorce her as long as he lives" (Deut. 22:29). Their perspective was a bit skewed, if you ask me. But that's the way it was in the Old Testament. The young girl who had sex out of wedlock was spoiled goods. Consequently, her father would have a terrible time finding another man to marry her. Think of it in terms of "you break it; you buy it." Not only did the man have to buy her, but he could never return her. She obviously had no protection from his continuing abuse.

We define adultery today as the violation of the marriage vows—specifically the promise to be sexually faithful to one's spouse. Either partner can be unfaithful because both are seen as equal participants in the marriage contract. But this was not the case in the Old Testament. Only the wife could be guilty of such a charge. It was impossible for a man to violate his own marriage. How could that be? It all had to do with property rights.

If a married woman had sex with a single or married man, she committed adultery by violating her husband's right to sole use of his property and the right to know for sure he fathered the children she bore. If he even suspected she was involved with another man, he could bring his wife before the priest. The priest mixed up a bitter batch of holy water and wrote curses on a scroll. The accused had to drink some of the bitter water. If she was innocent, nothing would happen to her body. But if her abdomen swelled and her thighs wasted away, the curses and bitter water would have disclosed her unfaithfulness. If she was found guilty, she was put to death.

If a married man had sex with an unmarried, unbetrothed woman, it would be seen as him taking her on as another wife. As mentioned previously, even if it was viewed as rape, he'd pay the father for the woman, marry her, and lose his divorce rights. If a married man had sex with a slave, a prostitute, a concubine, or a divorced or widowed woman, he was, again, not guilty of violating his own marriage. If, however, a married man had sex with a married woman, he was guilty of violating the property rights of the woman's husband. Both the man, single or married, and the married woman were put to death.

An engaged woman was considered to be the property of her husband-to-be and was, before the law, essentially a married woman. If a man had sex with a girl who was engaged, guilt and punishment were determined by the location of the encounter. If they had sex inside the city walls, it was assumed that it was consensual since she didn't cry out so someone could rescue her. Since she was already considered to be her betrothed husband's property, she was guilty of adultery. Her lover was guilty of violating her husband's property rights. They were both taken outside the city and stoned to death.

If the sexual encounter occurred in the country, the engaged woman was given the benefit of the doubt. The woman would have had no assistance in resisting the man's sexual advances, so she would be set free. The man, however, was held accountable for violating property rights and put to death.

Ownership but Not Total Control

Property ownership was not seen, however, as unfettered control over resources and people. Patriarchs were commanded by law to give one-tenth of their harvests and livestock to God. This offering, called a tithe, served several purposes. First, it reminded the Jews of the words in Genesis asserting that, ultimately, God was the grand Creator and therefore Owner of all the earth—the patriarchs included. Human beings were to multiply and manage the earth, not to mistakenly think they were indeed genuine "owners" of the planet.

The tithe offering was also meant to show gratitude to God for blessings given to the Jews and their ancestors. An expression of thanksgiving accompanied the giving of the tithe. A portion of the tithe went to the tribe of Levites who served as priests for the entire Jewish population. Since their efforts did not produce income per se, the tithes were meant to support their necessary spiritual contribution. Lastly, the tithe was to instill a compassion for the poor. Deuteronomy 26:12 reads, "When you have finished setting aside a tenth of all your produce in the third year, the year of the tithe, you shall give it to the Levite, the alien, the fatherless and the widow, so that they may eat in your towns and be satisfied."

In addition to specific tithes, the prosperous were directed to leave a portion of their harvest for the poor.

> When you are harvesting in your field and you overlook a sheaf, do not go back to get it. Leave it for the alien, the fatherless and the widow, so that the LORD your God may bless you in all the work of your hands. When you beat the olives from your trees, do not go over the branches a second time. Leave what remains for the alien, the fatherless and the widow. When you harvest the grapes in your vineyard, do not go over the vines again. Leave what remains for the alien, the fatherless and the widow. Remember that you were slaves in Egypt. That is why I command you to do this. (Deut. 24:19–22)

A general sense of compassion for those who are less fortunate was encouraged by instructions such as "Do not deprive the alien or the fatherless of justice, or take the cloak of the widow as a pledge. Remember that you were slaves in Egypt and the LORD your God redeemed you from there. That is why I command you to do this" (Deut. 24:17–18). And,

> Do not take advantage of a hired worker who is poor and
> needy, whether that worker is an Israelite or is a foreigner resid-
> ing in one of your towns. Pay them their wages each day before
> sunset, because they are poor and are counting on it. Otherwise
> they may cry to the LORD against you, and you will be guilty of
> sin. (Deut. 24:14–15 TNIV)

DIRTINESS

Purity and the practices that made one clean or unclean cannot be under-estimated in Jewish Law. A person was either clean or dirty at any given moment. A clean person tried his or her best to stay clean. If an individual did something to get dirty, specific remedies were outlined so that he could get cleaned up. Unfortunately, from time to time, people could participate in a practice that was so dirty that they were either exiled or executed. I imagine most tried to steer clear of those activities.

The body was a center of most of the purity laws. Generally speaking, one was made unclean by three body-related occurrences: what went into, what was on, or what came out of one's body. On the "going in" side, Jewish Law was very specific about what could be eaten and what could not. Some foods were clean and others were not. What was on a person's body, specifically one's skin, was also a clean/unclean consideration. The spread of infectious skin diseases and other diseases was of great concern to the Israelites. Separating people with con-tagious illnesses from the general population could be a matter of life and death for a community. The Law contains specific guidelines on dealing with these dis-eases and what procedure must be followed to declare them healed and, there-fore, clean. "Going out" concerns focused on bodily discharges of all sorts. A discharge could be caused by an illness, including sexually transmitted diseases. But what we would consider more natural discharges, such as semen, menstrual blood, or even having a baby could make one unclean. Let's look at some specific laws.

What Went into a Person's Body

Eating was a big deal. Here is a sampling of the laws outlining acceptable dietary practices:

> The LORD said to Moses, "Say to the Israelites: Do not eat any of the fat of cattle, sheep or goats. The fat of an animal found dead or torn by wild animals may be used for any other purpose, but you must not eat it. Anyone who eats the fat of an animal from which a food offering may be presented to the LORD must be cut off from their people. And wherever you live, you must not eat the blood of any bird or animal. Anyone who eats blood must be cut off from their people." (Lev. 7:22–27 TNIV)

Further in Leviticus, directives regarding eating are given—specifically restricting the eating of animals to those that both have a split hoof and chew cud:

> The LORD said to Moses and Aaron, "Say to the Israelites: 'Of all the animals that live on land, these are the ones you may eat: You may eat any animal that has a split hoof completely divided and that chews the cud. There are some that only chew the cud or only have a split hoof, but you must not eat them. The

camel, though it chews the cud, does not have a split hoof; it is ceremonially unclean for you. The coney, though it chews the cud, does not have a split hoof; it is unclean for you. The rabbit, though it chews the cud, does not have a split hoof; it is unclean for you. And the pig, though it has a split hoof completely divided, does not chew the cud; it is unclean for you. You must not eat their meat or touch their carcasses; they are unclean for you.'" (Lev. 11:1–8)

As for fish and other creatures that live in streams and oceans, Moses instructed the Jews to

eat any that have fins and scales. But all creatures in the seas or streams that do not have fins and scales—whether among all the swarming things or among all the other living creatures in the water—you are to detest. And since you are to detest them, you must not eat their meat and you must detest their carcasses. Anything living in the water that does not have fins and scales is to be detestable to you. (Lev. 11:9–12)

The Law goes on to list birds, insects, and other animals that are forbidden as legitimate food.

What Was on a Person's Body

A person could be made unclean not only by what *went into* the body, but by what *was on* the body. One avenue to uncleanness was touching someone or something that was already unclean. In continuation of the dietary laws, anyone who touched a dead animal became unclean. If an unclean animal died and fell on something owned by an Israelite, "that article, whatever its use, will be unclean, whether it is made of wood, cloth, hide or sackcloth. Put it in water; it will be unclean till evening, and then it will be clean" (Lev. 11:32). If a dead animal fell into a clay pot, the pot was to be broken. "Any food that could be eaten but has water on it from such a pot is unclean, and any liquid that could be drunk from it is unclean" (Lev. 11:34). Touching an article of clothing or a piece of furniture that was previously "contaminated" by an unclean person also made one unclean.

What was on the skin could also make a person unclean. The Law of Moses gave detailed descriptions of how infectious skin diseases should be dealt with. Before a person with a skin disorder could move freely in Jewish society, the priest had to examine him or her. In the meantime, "anyone with such a disease must wear torn clothes, let their hair be unkempt, cover the lower part of their face and cry out, 'Unclean! Unclean!' As long as they have the disease they remain unclean. They must live alone; they must live outside the camp" (Lev. 13:45–46 TNIV). Their fear of infectious disease is understandable, but we see things differently today. We provide treatment for the ill. Back then they were exiled without support or care.

What Came out of a Person's Body

Just about anything that came out of a person's body was thought of as unclean, making the person unclean at the same time. A man was considered unclean every time he ejaculated—whether he had sexual contact with a woman or not. "When a man has an emission of semen, he must bathe his whole body with water, and he will be unclean till evening. Any clothing or leather that has semen on it must be washed with water, and it will be unclean till evening" (Lev. 15:16–17).

Deuteronomy 23:10–11 reads, "If one of your men is unclean because of a nocturnal emission, he is to go outside the camp and stay there. But as evening approaches he is to wash himself, and at sunset he may return to the camp." Standing outside of camp for the day . . . everyone must have known why . . . how embarrassing was that?

When a man and a woman had sex, the man's semen caused both of them to be unclean. "When a man lies with a woman and there is an emission of semen, both must bathe with water, and they will be unclean till evening" (Lev. 15:18). Sex involving male orgasm dirties both parties.

Most of us today would not be judgmental about a menstruating woman (unless she was particularly crabby and then you might hear a complaint). But generally speaking, we view a woman's period as a natural part of being female. But according to Jewish Law, a woman was unclean for "seven days, and anyone who touches her will be unclean till evening" (Lev. 15:19). I can't imagine announcing to the world, "Hey, I'm on my period. Consider me unclean!" Apparently Jewish women gave some indication of their condition so that people could avoid touching them and thereby becoming unclean themselves. This included a woman's children and certainly her husband.

Having sex with a woman while she was on her period was a considerable offense. In Leviticus 20:18 we read, "If a man lies with a woman during her monthly period and has sexual relations with her, he has exposed the source of her flow, and she has also uncovered it. Both of them must be cut off from their people." Quite a stiff penalty for something we don't think twice about today. Some couples may prefer to refrain from sex at this time, but I've never heard a sermon preached against it. This "offense" doesn't register on our Sin Richter Scale.

If "what was coming out" of a woman's body was a baby, she was more unclean if she gave birth to a daughter than to a son. If a woman gave birth to a girl, she was dirty for two weeks. If she gave birth to a boy, it was shortened to one week. She was then to wait a specific period of time (depending on the gender of her newborn) before appearing before a priest and providing a specified animal offering, whereby he would offer the animals to the Lord to make atonement for her. She needed "atonement" for giving birth. Amazing. Once this was accomplished, "then she will be ceremonially clean from her flow of blood" (Lev. 12:7). Again, it wouldn't occur to any of us today to consider a woman unclean who has just given birth. These days, everyone is invited into the delivery room and the whole process is videotaped.

PRACTICES

For many in the church, in the past and today as well, sex isn't viewed as a good and decent activity—period. Over the years, this idea has been taken to the extreme. Living a sexless life has been elevated as spiritually superior to a sexually active one by some Christian leaders. Indeed, parts of Christendom have argued passionately in favor of celibacy and against any form of sexual activity, even within the parameters of a committed marital relationship.

Additionally, Mosaic Law spoke out against practices that didn't necessarily fall into the two previous categories. One was prostitution. This probably comes as no surprise. Patriarchs were responsible for financially supporting the women under their care, making sure that they did not have to resort to prostitution for economic reasons. Jewish fathers were not to prostitute their daughters or sell them to those who would. Prostitution was also linked with idol worship, which was severely rejected. "No Israelite man or woman is to become a shrine prostitute. You may not bring the earnings of a female prostitute or of a male prostitute into the house of the LORD your God to pay any vow, because the LORD your God detests them both" (Deut. 23:17–18).

Cross-dressing was also a no-no. "A woman must not wear men's clothing, nor a man wear women's clothing, for the LORD your God detests anyone who does this" (Deut. 22:5).

I've left my favorite for last. Be careful what you touch . . . "If two men are fighting and the wife of one of them comes to rescue her husband from his assailant, and she reaches out and seizes him by his private parts, you shall cut off her hand. Show her no pity" (Deut. 25:11–12). I have no idea how often this must have happened in ancient Israel, but apparently there were enough incidents that a law was needed to put a stop to it.

Property rights, purity, and practices are three aspects of sexuality addressed in Scripture. We've begun our exploration in the Old Testament and will continue in the next chapter to see what Jesus and the New Testament writers had to say. We'll see if Jesus and the church maintained and extended these Jewish laws for believers, or if Old Testament laws were redefined or even contradicted.

Chapter 2

Jesus Defies Convention

I t's not uncommon to hear historians, philosophers, and even theologians marvel at how one man from an obscure part of the Roman Empire could impact the entire world. And yet if you take the time to actually read what Jesus taught and see how he behaved, it's little wonder that, should his words be taken seriously, the status quo would be fundamentally challenged.

When Jesus was born, the Jews saw themselves as unique from and superior to other cultures because of the rigorous way they kept the Law and carried on Jewish tradition from one generation to the next. As mentioned in the previous chapter, the family was the primary building block of the society and the glue that held it all together.

JESUS AND PROPERTY RIGHTS

Jesus did not address property rights directly. He did however challenge the existing conceptions of what made up a family. He elevated our responsibility to God over family, redefined the spiritual ideal, elevated the dignity of women, distributed power equally within marriage, and empowered the individual to make personal choices.

> → To say that we are called to preach holiness or sanctification, is to get into a side eddy. We are called to proclaim Jesus Christ. The fact that He saves from sin and makes us holy is part of the effect of the wonderful abandonment of God. Abandonment never produces the consciousness of its own effort, because the whole life is taken up with the One to Whom we abandon.[1]

Jesus Redefines the Family

When Jesus called his twelve disciples, he wasn't picking out men who were footloose and fancy-free. Tradition tells us most of the disciples were married—except perhaps John, because he was so young. For example, evidence of Peter's family is mentioned in Matthew 8:14–15: "When Jesus came into Peter's house, he saw Peter's mother-in-law lying in bed with a fever. He touched her hand and the fever left her, and she got up and began to wait on him." Just because the disciples' wives weren't mentioned by name in the New Testament does not support the idea that they were single. Nor does it suppose they were childless. In fact, it was probable that they were married and also probable that most of them had children. Jewish men were also responsible for extended families, such as the care of aging parents. It was taken for granted. It was the Jewish way.

But Jesus pitted Jewish family values against the cost of discipleship. They were to immediately set their professions and family responsibilities aside and follow him. For example, Matthew 4:18–22 reads:

> As Jesus was walking beside the Sea of Galilee, he saw two brothers, Simon called Peter and his brother Andrew. They were casting a net into the lake, for they were fishermen. "Come, follow me," Jesus said, "and I will send you out to fish for people." At once they left their nets and followed him.
>
> Going on from there, he saw two other brothers, James son of Zebedee and his brother John. They were in a boat with their father Zebedee, preparing their nets. Jesus called them, and immediately they left the boat and their father and followed him. (TNIV)

In light of what we know about Jewish culture, Jesus's insistence that his followers abandon everything, especially one's duties to one's father and family, was outrageous. He transferred their primary responsibility from the traditional family to service to God. And he didn't make this point softly:

> Anyone who loves their father and mother more than me is not worthy of me; anyone who loves their son or daughter more than me is not worthy of me. Whoever does not take up their cross and follow me is not worthy of me. Whoever finds their

life will lose it, and whoever loses their life for my sake will find

it. (Matt. 10:37–39 TNIV)

Jesus required his disciples to put faith into action by immediately following him, not after arrangements were made. It is possible that some of the disciples grabbed their wives and children, bringing them along for the trip. I suspect this was the case, as it is mentioned more than once in the Gospels that Jesus traveled with large crowds. But even if the families came along, serving Jesus was top priority—a clear departure from the traditional Jewish social structure.

Jesus not only expected his followers to put him in front of their families, he did so himself. Matthew tells this story:

While Jesus was still talking to the crowd, his mother and brothers stood outside, wanting to speak to him. Someone told him, "Your mother and brothers are standing outside, wanting to speak to you."

He replied to him, "Who is my mother, and who are my brothers?" Pointing to his disciples, he said, "Here are my mother and my brothers. For whoever does the will of my Father in heaven is my brother and sister and mother." (Matt. 12:46–50)

Calling fellow Christians "brothers and sisters in Christ" may be cliché to us, but to the Jews of Jesus's time, this idea was utterly foreign. The Old Testament view of the family, and whom one would treat as family, was clearly defined. Only blood relatives or those bound by marriage were included.

Jesus's declaration that a shared faith was the determining factor of familial connection was a clear challenge to traditional Jewish Law.

Jesus Redefines the Spiritual Ideal

Males were seen as spiritually superior to females and adults superior to children. In those days, much as we do today, people looked up to their spiritual leaders as having an authority and understanding the average person may not have. And, much like today, these leaders came to believe that they were, indeed, spiritually superior to the rest of the crowd. But Jesus would have none of the pomp and circumstance. He offended many when "little children were brought to Jesus for him to place his hands on them and pray for them. But the disciples rebuked those who brought them. Jesus said, 'Let the little children come to me, and do not hinder them, for the kingdom of heaven belongs to such as these'" (Matt. 19:13–14). Jesus reversed the pecking order by declaring that children (commonly seen as property, spiritually inferior to adult males, and essentially last in line) have ownership in the kingdom of heaven. This couldn't have made Jewish leaders, or even the average male, all that happy.

Jesus Redefines the Dignity of Women

Jesus was constantly surprising his disciples by the way he interacted with women. Men were not to have public contact with women of any status— married or single, Jewish or Gentile, old or young. And yet Jesus violated this standard repeatedly. He initiated contact with a Samaritan woman (thereby contradicting both gender and racial codes) by asking her to give him a drink from a well (John 4:7–42). He included women in his entourage, choosing to show himself first to Mary Magdalene after his resurrection and then to his male disciples.

Jesus Redefines Power in Marriage

One of the most unpopular themes of Jesus's teaching (at least among the men) was in regard to marriage and divorce. The men in Jesus's audience were accustomed to owning their wives and children, with the right to divorce at their discretion. Jesus put the kibosh on that idea.

> Some Pharisees came to him to test him. They asked, "Is it lawful for a man to divorce his wife for any and every reason?"
>
> "Haven't you read," he replied, "that at the beginning the Creator 'made them male and female,' and said, 'For this reason a man will leave his father and mother and be united to his wife, and the two will become one flesh'? So they are no longer two, but one. Therefore what God has joined together, let no one separate."
>
> "Why then," they asked, "did Moses command that a man give his wife a certificate of divorce and send her away?"
>
> Jesus replied, "Moses permitted you to divorce your wives because your hearts were hard. But it was not this way from the beginning. I tell you that anyone who divorces his wife, except for sexual immorality, and marries another woman commits adultery." (Matt. 19:3–9 TNIV)

I want to interrupt this story here to point out that, according to Jewish Law, it was impossible for a man to violate his marital vows. Jesus was saying, "Sorry, guys, but you are as responsible to the marriage as your wife is." He was implying that a man should not take on more than one wife—eliminating the option for a man to simply "marry" a woman with whom he had sex. He was to have one wife and remain sexually faithful to her. And unless she was unfaithful to him, he was not allowed to divorce her. This was a huge blow to Jewish men who heard Jesus teach.

His disciples put two and two together and said, "If this is the situation between a husband and wife, it is better not to marry" (Matt. 19:10). In other words, if we can't be in charge and be free of a particular woman whenever we please, why would we make a marital commitment in the first place?

> A fellow and a girl who wed
> Begin to live as one 'tis said,
> But many couples can't agree
> Which one of them they wish to be.

"Jesus replied, 'Not everyone can accept this word, but only those to whom it has been given.'" For those who chose not to marry? They were to remain celibate. Jesus continued, "For some are eunuchs because they were born that way; others have been made eunuchs; and others have renounced marriage because of the kingdom of heaven. The one who can accept this should accept it" (Matt. 19:11–12 TNIV).

Wow! Men and women were equally bound to the marital relationship. Divorce was permitted when one of the partners violated that commitment. And if you didn't want to share power in your marriage, then stay single . . . the way a eunuch is single.

Jesus Redefines the Role of the Individual

Perhaps the most profound element of Jesus's teachings was the fact that he spoke directly to individuals. He did not approach a person as if he or she were owned by someone else—but as an individual, free and responsible to make personal choices. By doing so, he redefined the primary social unit to be the individual person, not the family unit. If applied, the foundation of the

Jewish culture would be altered in such a radical way as to make the Old Testament Law impossible to apply. Jesus's ideas altered Western society and a good bit of Eastern society as well.

Jesus Redefines a Giving Heart

Jewish Law called upon those who had wealth to share it with those who were less fortunate. At least 10 percent of one's holdings were to go to support the temple and to the needy (who included non-Jews traveling in Jewish areas, orphans, and widows). Jesus was not impressed with the symbolic giving in which many of the religious leaders of his day engaged. He caustically declared in Matthew 23:23–24, "Woe to you, teachers of the law and Pharisees, you hypocrites! You give a tenth of your spices—mint, dill and cumin. But you have neglected the more important matters of the law—justice, mercy and faithfulness. You should have practiced the latter, without neglecting the former. You blind guides! You strain out a gnat but swallow a camel" (TNIV).

JESUS AND PURITY

Jesus personally acted in ways and taught ideas that seemed to violate current applications of the Law. This usually upset people. Once gaining their attention, however, Jesus pointed out the underlying principle conveyed through the Law.

Jesus Touched the Untouchable

Jewish Law forbade Jews from associating with a variety of people: they could not enter Gentiles' homes or eat with them; men could not publicly converse with women; the physically healthy could not come into contact with the sick; respectable Jews were not to mix with the likes of tax collectors or prostitutes. Jesus not only associated with everyone he wasn't "supposed" to; he also did something even more shocking to the Jewish community. He actually touched unclean people and allowed them to touch him.

If you touched someone who was "unclean," then you became unclean as well. Beyond reasons of the Law, most people steered clear of people with diseases out of fear of contagion. This was extremely so with leprosy. Transmission of the disease terrified people, so lepers were divided from their families and society. Jesus healed many of the disease and could have healed one particular man without physical contact, but that's not the way he chose to change lives. He, by the letter of the Law, made himself unclean in the process of ridding a man of his illness.

> While Jesus was in one of the towns, a man came along who was covered with leprosy. When he saw Jesus, he fell with his face to the ground and begged him, "Lord, if you are willing, you can make me clean."
>
> Jesus reached out his hand and touched the man. "I am willing," he said. "Be clean!" And immediately the leprosy left him.
>
> Then Jesus ordered him, "Don't tell anyone, but go, show yourself to the priest and offer the sacrifices that Moses commanded for your cleansing, as a testimony to them." (Luke 5:12–14)

As you can see, Jesus instructed the man to follow through with Jewish cleansing laws. At the same time, he did not consider himself unclean, even though the Law would have judged him so. Jesus's behavior supported the Law and defied the rules at the same time.

Jesus Allowed the Untouchable to Touch Him

We have several stories in which people touched Jesus, usually without his permission. However, in one instance, Jesus allowed a woman to touch him in public, and touch him for an extended period of time. This, of course, was scandalous in his day. She was, first of all, a woman. Second, she was a woman "who had lived a sinful life." While Jesus was visiting the house of a Pharisee, this woman "brought an alabaster jar of perfume, and as she stood behind him at his feet weeping, she began to wet his feet with her tears. Then she wiped them with her hair, kissed them and poured perfume on them" (Luke 7:37–38). Of course this freaked everyone out. I even think that if something like this happened today, it would throw us off balance. How many times have you invited a pastor over for dinner and some strange woman dropped in and cried all over, kissed, and perfumed his feet? All I'm saying is that there'd be talk.

Jesus Criticized Religious Hypocrites

Jesus was extremely critical of religious leaders who played the Jewish purity game but were, in their hearts, selfish and cruel. A sampling of his condemnation can be found in Matthew 23:25–28:

> Woe to you, teachers of the law and Pharisees, you hypocrites! You clean the outside of the cup and dish, but inside they are full of greed and self-indulgence. Blind Pharisee! First clean the inside of the cup and dish, and then the outside also will be clean.
>
> Woe to you, teachers of the law and Pharisees, you hypocrites! You are like whitewashed tombs, which look beautiful on the outside but on the inside are full of the bones of the dead and everything unclean. In the same way, on the outside you appear

to people as righteous but on the inside you are full of hypocrisy and wickedness. (TNIV)

Jesus Expanded the Definition of Sexual Sin

Jesus spoke to the heart of sexual impropriety when he said in Matthew 5:27–28, "You have heard that it is said, 'Do not commit adultery.' But I tell you that anyone who looks at a woman lustfully has already committed adultery with her in his heart."

Yeow! There's an upsetting thought to someone who has built his or her identity and social standing on rule keeping. You wouldn't want to hear that your impeccable behavior wasn't enough to satisfy God. You'd be resistant to the idea that you were accountable not merely for your actions, but for your thoughts as well. Some Christians have taken these words of Jesus to mean that any sexual feeling or impulse is sinful. Others, with whom I agree (so they must be right), interpret this to mean that one is accountable for the monitoring of one's sexual fantasy life. I want to make the point here that the internal workings of one's sexual life are just as important as impeccable behavior.

Jesus Contradicted Purity Laws Related to Eating

Jewish Law clearly restricted the eating habits of its followers. Specific foods were considered clean and unclean. How these foods were to be eaten was also a matter of tradition. One was to eat "clean" foods with "clean" hands. But Jesus blew all of this out of the water when he taught that a person is not clean or unclean according to what is eaten, nor how it is eaten.

Jesus called the crowd to him and said, "Listen and understand. What goes into a man's mouth does not make you 'unclean,' but what comes out of his mouth, that is what makes him 'unclean.'"

Then the disciples came to him and asked, "Do you know that the Pharisees were offended when they heard this?"

He replied, "Every plant that my heavenly Father has not planted will be pulled up by the roots. Leave them; they are blind guides. If a blind man leads a blind man, both will fall into a pit."

Peter said, "Explain the parable to us."

"Are you still so dull?" Jesus asked. "Don't you see that whatever enters the mouth goes into the stomach and then out of the body? But the things that come out of the mouth come from the heart, and these make a man 'unclean.' For out of the heart come evil thoughts, murder, adultery, sexual immorality, theft, false testimony, slander. These are what make a man 'unclean'; but eating with unwashed hands does not make him 'unclean.'" (Matt. 15:10–20)

JESUS AND SEXUAL PRACTICES

It's not easy to know for sure what Jesus believed about specific sexual practices. He addressed his comments regarding sex, in general, to married men who had misused their power by arbitrarily divorcing their wives. Sex and power, for Jesus, were closely tied. He also redirected attention from the observance of specific rules to a person's intention. Jesus made no direct comments about specific kinds of sexual activity, although some believe he did so metaphorically.

→ Did Jesus Speak Metaphorically About Masturbation?

Some Jewish and Christian scholars think that Jesus made reference to masturbation in Matthew 5:30 when he said, "And if your right hand causes you to sin, cut it off and throw it away. It is better for you to lose one part of your body than for your whole body to go into hell."

Here is the verse in context, Matthew 5:29–30:

If your right eye causes you to sin, gouge it out and throw it away. It is better for you to lose one part of your body than for your whole body to be thrown into hell. And if your right hand causes you to sin, cut it off and throw it away. It is better for you to lose one part of your body than for your whole body to go into hell.

I personally see Jesus speaking metaphorically about the importance of our priorities—that nothing is more important than our commitment to God. I do not believe that Jesus was instructing people to literally gouge out their eyes or cut off their hands.

For those who want to put these two verses into a sexual

> > >

> > >

context, let me quote the preceding verses, 27–28, "You have heard that it was said, 'Do not commit adultery.' But I tell you that anyone who looks at a woman lustfully has already committed adultery with her in his heart." Perhaps Jesus was telling us that if we lust with our eyes or touch people we should not be intimate with, we commit a serious sin . . . so serious, that it would metaphorically result in the loss of our ability to see or touch anyone at all.

Chapter 3

Was Paul Purposely Trying to Confuse Us?

To understand the context in which the New Testament church developed and to more accurately interpret Scripture, it is essential to get a view of the overriding context—Roman values and laws. The Romans took pride in their ability to conquer every culture with whom they came in contact. Showing mercy was not a virtue.

Roman citizens carried this capacity into their personal lives, using the oppression of others as a way to elevate one's standing in the community. In fact, Romans were entertained by the suffering of others, as illustrated by their attendance at the gladiator spectacles and watching people, sometimes Christians, be torn to pieces by wild animals. We also have remnants of their plays that used the humiliation and suffering of defenseless people as humorous, rather than tragic, events.

This rather gruff society was divided into two parts: the free and the slave, the intimidator and the intimidated. At the time Christianity was first introduced to the Roman Empire, it is estimated that from one-fourth to one-third of the entire population was composed of slaves. Slaves were property, not persons, who were either born to the status or captured by Roman soldiers through military conquests. From time to time, slaves were given their freedom by their masters, but there was nothing slaves could do to earn freedom. Release from slavery was at the discretion of their master. Slave owners had all but total power over their slaves and could whip, beat, and humiliate them for any reason whatsoever.

Against this rather brutal background, we find a similar, although hopefully softer, relationship between the sexes. The image of the ideal Roman family resonated in the minds of many of its citizens, somewhat like a Norman Rockwell painting triggers our longings for an idealized America that has never quite existed. The ideal family was a husband, flanked by a loving wife and adoring children.

→ How the New Testament Came to Be

The Bible we use today is comprised of the Old and the New Testaments. When Jesus referred to the Scriptures, he meant the writings in the Old Testament. The New Testament wasn't written, gathered, and agreed upon until years after Jesus left this earth. In fact, the books included in the New Testament weren't finalized until 393 at the Synod of Hippo—nearly four hundred years after Jesus's birth.

But on a realistic basis, the culture tended to pit men *against* women in the area of romance, rather than draw them together. A man who genuinely loved his wife and showed any kind of affection toward her was seen as weak and "henpecked." For example, we have the writings of Seneca, a Stoic who became Nero's tutor in AD 50. (Fifteen years later, in AD 65, Nero forced Seneca to commit suicide because he thought Seneca had betrayed him.) Long before that fateful day, Seneca wrote:

All love for someone else's wife is shameful. But it is also shameful to love one's own wife immoderately. In loving his wife, the wise man takes reason for his guide, not emotion. He resists the assault of passions, and does not allow himself to be impetuously swept away into the marital act. Nothing is more depraved than to love one's spouse as if she were an adulteress.

In other words, the more emotionally and sexually distant a husband was from his wife, the more morally grounded he was. It is not surprising that a lonely wife, desperate for her husband's affection, is another regular theme in Roman theater.

Marriage in our society is regulated by the government. The Roman Empire did not regulate marriage as we are accustomed. Marital arrangements were made privately and, at times, were rather loosely defined. There were two kinds of marital agreements: one in which the woman became a member of her husband's family, under the authority of her husband, and the other in which she remained a member of her original family, under the authority of her father. The purpose of marriage was to produce heirs for the husband. As in Jewish culture, women were expected to marry young, although it was illegal for a girl to be given in marriage under the age of twelve. Since a wife's purpose was to give her husband children, some marriages weren't considered legitimate until the first child was born. The woman was supposed to marry as a virgin, but the husband was not held to the same standard.

Although Roman culture was rough around the edges, motherhood was esteemed and seen as a worthy role (albeit the only role) for women. If a woman proved especially fertile, she would probably enjoy a securer place in her husband's household. However, a mother had no legal right to her own children. Her husband had sole legal authority over his children, and he was free to discipline them or dispose of them as he chose. Adoption was a common practice in Roman culture, unlike Jewish tradition. A father could distribute his offspring to his brothers or other relatives to adopt as their own if he so chose.

Women who could not conceive fared poorly in Roman culture. They were expected to peacefully allow their husbands to divorce them and return to their homes of origin. The men were then free to remarry, hopefully finding a fertile woman, on his second (or third) time around. If an infertile woman stayed with her husband, she was to look the other way while her husband collected concubines or propagated heirs in less conventional means.

As with Jewish Law, divorce was an option for the husband, not the wife, although it was possible for the couple to separate by mutual agreement. In Jewish tradition, the husband had to provide the wife with a written decree. In the Roman Empire, the husband simply had to tell his wife he was divorcing her. It was also permitted for him to inform her by letter or by having a slave let her know she was being dismissed.

Widows were required by law to marry quickly after their husbands' deaths. Some widows were fined if they did not marry within two years. The legal concern was related to property rights; the state did not want a widow to remain in control of her late husband's estate. Once she remarried, whatever she owned became the property of her new husband. The culture was more accepting of male property owners than female.

As far as sexual activity in the empire, many scholars debunk the "wild Roman orgies" we have often heard about as being more fiction than fact. The paintings we have of such goings-on were probably more pornographic than historic. In fact, sex wasn't a proper topic for discussion for respectable Romans. As long as people kept their sex lives private and didn't cause a scandal, there wasn't much of a consequence. It was assumed that a man would not have sex with his wife when she was pregnant, and perhaps even for the year or two she was nursing. Meanwhile, it was fine for a man to have sex with his slaves—they were his to do with as he willed. Sex with prostitutes was also acceptable. But consensual sex with a free woman was considered adulterous, and punishment for adultery was death.

THE NEW TESTAMENT CHURCH
ON PROPERTY RIGHTS

As the New Testament church developed, no stand was taken against slavery or the ownership of wives or children. The church's stance on concubines is unclear. Alongside this acceptance of Roman social and legal norms, the church promoted values that did not comply with the status quo. The church began to see itself as a compassionate community, a place where people in need could find shelter, assistance, and justice. It was assumed that congregations would hold members accountable for upholding these new Christian values. Those in power, such as slave owners, husbands, and fathers, were to treat their slaves, wives, and children kindly, based in their love for Christ. Those without formal power, such as slaves, wives, and children, were instructed to be submissive to their masters, husbands, and fathers (although this last part wasn't anything particularly new).

The arrangement of marriages remained under the jurisdiction of families, not the state. But Christianity changed the internal workings of marriage. In the church, husbands were expected to be sexually faithful to their wives. Even though husbands still had the legal right to divorce their wives as granted by Roman law, the church expected Christian men not to exercise that right. Polygamy and incest were out—monogamy and fidelity were in. It was assumed that both bride and groom would be virgins on their wedding night, doing away with the double standard that required females to be chaste while males had sexual license. Being single rose in status, as being free of marital and family responsibilities gave more time for prayer and ministry. Consequently, it was acceptable for Christian teenage girls to put off marriage a few more years than their nonbelieving counterparts. In keeping with this value, widows were not forced to remarry but were cared for by the church if they had no extended family to assume their care.

Early Christians also modified their management of wealth where voluntary charity was encouraged. Initially, no one was expected to share wealth or property with other believers. People had bursts of generosity out of their love for other believers. Eventually, the early church became known for its acts of charity and sharing as this initial spontaneity grew into a shared value. Owning property was not seen as evil. However, amassing wealth for its own sake was not seen as virtuous. Those who had were expected to share with those who didn't.

A sense of responsibility to the poor that was first established in Old Testament Law was more fully developed in belief and action by the early church.

A SAMPLING OF PAUL'S WRITINGS ON PROPERTY RIGHTS

Paul is the most extensive writer regarding the roles Christians are to play within the church and society at large. Jewish values held marriage and procreation in the highest esteem. Paul, in contrast, elevates singlehood and celibacy to an all-time high. He encourages people not to marry and, if widowed, not to remarry. Marriage is seen as a solution for sexual desire that cannot be managed. At times, Paul seems to contradict himself. For example, he says that men must demonstrate their abilities to manage their own household of wife and children to qualify for church leadership. He also seems to promote competing ideas about women in leadership, as he commends specific women who are in ministry, while forbidding women to speak in church.

I suspect more theologians have argued over interpreting Paul's writings than any other single author of Scripture. Perhaps this can partially account for what appear to be discrepancies and contradictions in his writings. If you line many of them up (and I'm about to do that), you'll see that he doesn't promote one consistent perspective on issues such as marriage and body ownership. In the next section, we'll look at his views on celibacy, which tend to be more consistent. Most scholars believe Paul was married at some time in his life. We can only speculate if he was married during his travels and whether or not his wife accompanied him. We do know that Paul advocated singleness over married life. I've included the passages in the King James Version and the New International Version. You'll see how two translations can give different slants on the same passage.

Your Body Is a Member of the Body of Christ
1 Corinthians 12:12–14

For as the body is one, and hath many members, and all the members of that one body, being many, are one body: so also is Christ. For by one Spirit are we all baptized into one body, whether we be Jews or Gentiles, whether we be bond or free; and have been all made to drink into one Spirit. For the body is not one member, but many. (KJV)

The body is a unit, though it is made up of many parts; and though all its parts are many, they form one body. So it is with Christ. For we were all baptized by one Spirit into one body—whether Jews or Greeks, slave or free—and we were all given the one Spirit to drink.

Now the body is not made up of one part but of many. (NIV)

If You Can't Control Yourself, Go Ahead and Get Married

As for marriage, Paul wasn't the most enthusiastic.

1 Corinthians 7:1–2

Now concerning the things whereof ye wrote unto me: It is good for a man *not to touch a woman*. Nevertheless, to avoid fornication, let every man have his own wife, and let every woman have her own husband. (KJV, emphasis mine)

Now for the matters you wrote about: It is good for a man *not to marry*. But since there is so much immorality, each man should have his own wife, and each woman her own husband. (NIV, emphasis mine)

While I'm No Big Fan of Marriage, I'm Also Against People Who Forbid Others from Getting Married
1 Timothy 4:1–5

Now the Spirit speaketh expressly, that in the latter times some shall depart from the faith, giving heed to seducing spirits, and doctrines of devils; speaking lies in hypocrisy; having their conscience seared with a hot iron; forbidding to marry, and commanding to abstain from meats, which God hath created to be received with thanksgiving of them which believe and know the truth. For every creature of God is good, and nothing to be refused, if it be received with thanksgiving: for it is sanctified by the word of God and prayer. (KJV)

The Spirit clearly says that in later times some will abandon the faith and follow deceiving spirits and things taught by demons. Such teachings come through hypocritical liars, whose consciences have been seared as with a hot iron. They forbid people to marry and order them to abstain from certain foods, which God created to be received with thanksgiving by those who believe and who know the truth. For everything God created is good, and nothing is to be rejected if it is received with thanksgiving, because it is consecrated by the word of God and prayer. (NIV)

We're All Equal in Christ
Galatians 3:26–28

For ye are all the children of God by faith in Christ Jesus. For as many

So in Christ Jesus you are all children of God through faith, for of you as have been baptized into Christ have put on Christ. There is neither Jew nor Greek, there is neither bond nor free, there is neither male nor female: for ye are all one in Christ Jesus. (KJV)

all of you who were baptized into Christ have clothed yourselves with Christ. There is neither Jew nor Greek, neither slave nor free, neither male nor female, for you are all one in Christ Jesus. (TNIV)

Model Your Marriage After Christ and the Church
Ephesians 5:21–33

. . . submitting yourselves one to another in the fear of God. Wives, submit yourselves unto your own husbands, as unto the Lord. For the husband is the head of the wife, even as Christ is the head of the church: and he is the saviour of the body. Therefore as the church is subject unto Christ, so let the wives be to their own husbands in every thing.

Husbands, love your wives, even as Christ also loved the church, and gave himself for it; that he might sanctify and cleanse it with the washing of water by the word, that he might present it to himself a glorious church, not having spot, or

Submit to one another out of reverence for Christ.

Wives, submit yourselves to your own husbands as to the Lord. For the husband is the head of the wife as Christ is the head of the church, his body, of which he is the Savior. Now as the church submits to Christ, so also wives should submit to their husbands in everything.

Husbands, love your wives, just as Christ loved the church and gave himself up for her to make her holy, cleansing her by the washing with water through the word, and to present her to himself as a wrinkle, or any such thing; but that it should be holy and without blemish. So ought men to love their wives as their own bodies. He that loveth his wife loveth himself. For no man ever yet hated his own flesh; but nourisheth and cherisheth it, even as the Lord the church: For we are members of his body, of his flesh, and of his bones. For this cause shall a man leave his father and mother, and shall be joined unto his wife, and they two shall be one flesh. This is a great mystery: but I speak concerning Christ and the church. Nevertheless let every one of you in particular so love his wife even as himself; and the wife see that she reverence her husband. (KJV)

radiant church, without stain or wrinkle or any other blemish, but holy and blameless. In this same way, husbands ought to love their wives as their own bodies. He who loves his wife loves himself. After all, people have never hated their own bodies, but they feed and care for them, just as Christ does the church—for we are members of his body. "For this reason a man will leave his father and mother and be united to his wife, and the two will become one flesh." This is a profound mystery—but I am talking about Christ and the church. However, each one of you also must love his wife as he loves himself, and the wife must respect her husband. (TNIV)

And Remember, If You Do Get Married, Your Body Belongs to Your Spouse, and Vice Versa
1 Corinthians 7:3–7

Let the husband render unto the wife due benevolence: and likewise also the wife unto the husband. *The*

The husband should fulfill his marital duty to his wife, and likewise the wife to her husband. *The wife*

wife hath not power of her own body, but the husband: and likewise also *the husband hath not power of his own body,* but the wife. Defraud ye not one the other, except it be with consent for a time, that ye may give yourselves to fasting and prayer; and come together again, that Satan tempt you not for your incontinency. But I speak this by permission, and not of commandment. For I would that all men were even as I myself. But every man hath his proper gift of God, one after this manner, and another after that. (KJV, emphasis mine)

does not have authority over her own body but yields it to her husband. In the same way, *the husband does not have authority over his own body* but yields it to his wife. Do not deprive each other except perhaps by mutual consent and for a time, so that you may devote yourselves to prayer. Then come together again so that Satan will not tempt you because of your lack of self-control. I say this as a concession, not as a command. I wish that all of you were as I am. But each of you has your own gift from God; one has this gift, another has that. (TNIV, emphasis mine)

A SAMPLE OF PAUL'S WRITINGS ON PURITY

We Christians seem to be comfortable with body-related and even sexually related metaphors. We're always talking about the church as being the "body of Christ" or the "bride of Christ." Husbands are to love their wives as Christ loved the church, comparing the marital relationship with the relationship Christ has with us. We're for body talk as long as it's symbolic.

When it comes to our actual bodies, Christian discourse takes a dramatic turn toward blame. We have pointed to our bodies, sometimes referred to as "flesh," as the source of sin. Due, in part, to translation problems, our physical bodies and our sinful natures have been seen as synonymous. But let's be honest here. It's not our legs' fault when we go places we shouldn't or our hands' fault for touching people in ways we shouldn't have touched. It's *our* fault. It seems like a way to avoid responsibility when we blame our bodies, even our sexual desire, for the sin we may have committed. And yet these concepts seem to be intertwined in the following passages.

Your Flesh Is a Source of Sin
Romans 7:5–6

For when we were in the flesh, the motions of sins, which were by the law, did work in our members to bring forth fruit unto death. But now we are delivered from the law, that being dead wherein we were held; that we should serve in newness of spirit, and not in the oldness of the letter. (KJV)

For when we were controlled by the sinful nature, the sinful passions aroused by the law were at work in our bodies, so that we bore fruit for death. But now, by dying to what once bound us, we have been released from the law so that we serve in the new way of the Spirit, and not in the old way of the written code. (NIV)

Romans 7:18

For I know that in me (that is, in my flesh,) dwelleth no good thing: for to will is present with me; but how to perform that which is good I find not. (KJV)

I know that nothing good lives in me, that is, in my sinful nature. For I have the desire to do what is good, but I cannot carry it out. (NIV)

And Yet, Jesus Is Manifested in Your Body
2 Corinthians 4:7–11

But we have this treasure in earthen vessels, that the excellency of the power may be of God, and not of us. We are troubled on every side, yet not distressed; we are perplexed, but not in despair; persecuted, but not forsaken; cast down, but not destroyed; always bearing about in the body the dying of the Lord Jesus, that the life also of Jesus might be made manifest in our body. For we which live are always delivered unto death for Jesus' sake, that the life also of Jesus might be made manifest in our mortal flesh. (KJV)

But we have this treasure in jars of clay to show that this all-surpassing power is from God and not from us. We are hard pressed on every side, but not crushed; perplexed, but not in despair; persecuted, but not abandoned; struck down, but not destroyed. We always carry around in our body the death of Jesus, so that the life of Jesus may also be revealed in our body. For we who are alive are always being given over to death for Jesus' sake, so that his life may be revealed in our mortal body. (NIV)

A SAMPLE OF PAUL'S WRITINGS ON PRACTICES

Paul urged Christians of his day to live orderly, harmonious, and sober lives. He emphasized repeatedly that our sexual behavior is important to God. Believers are to be single and celibate or married and sexually intimate. Paul's comments about any specific sexual activity fall outside the parameters of these guidelines. The context of sexual activity, rather than the activity itself, seems to be important to Paul.

Behave Yourselves
Romans 13:13

Let us walk honestly, as in the day; not in rioting and drunkenness, not in chambering and wantonness, not in strife and envying. (KJV)

Let us behave decently, as in the daytime, not in orgies and drunkenness, not in sexual immorality and debauchery, not in dissension and jealousy. (NIV)

What You Do with Your Body Matters
Romans 6:11–14

Likewise reckon ye also yourselves to be dead indeed unto sin, but alive unto God through Jesus Christ our Lord. Let not sin therefore reign in your mortal body, that ye should obey it in the lusts thereof. Neither yield ye your members as instruments of unrighteousness unto sin: but yield yourselves unto God, as those that are alive from the dead, and your members as instruments of righteousness unto God. For sin shall not have dominion over you: for ye are not under the law, but under grace. (KJV)

In the same way, count yourselves dead to sin but alive to God in Christ Jesus. Therefore do not let sin reign in your mortal body so that you obey its evil desires. Do not offer the parts of your body to sin, as instruments of wickedness, but rather offer yourselves to God, as those who have been brought from death to life; and offer the parts of your body to him as instruments of righteousness. For sin shall not be your master, because you are not under law, but under grace. (NIV)

And What You Talk About Is Important Too
Ephesians 5:1–5

Be ye therefore followers of God, as dear children; and walk in love, as Christ also hath loved us, and hath given himself for us an offering and a sacrifice to God for a sweetsmelling savour. But fornication, and all uncleanness, or covetousness, let it not be once named among you, as becometh saints; neither filthiness, nor foolish talking, nor jesting, which are not convenient: but rather giving of thanks. For this ye know, that no whoremonger, nor unclean person, nor covetous man, who is an idolater, hath any inheritance in the kingdom of Christ and of God. (KJV)

Be imitators of God, therefore, as dearly loved children and live a life of love, just as Christ loved us and gave himself up for us as a fragrant offering and sacrifice to God.

But among you there must not be even a hint of sexual immorality, or of any kind of impurity, or of greed, because these are improper for God's holy people. Nor should there be obscenity, foolish talk or coarse joking, which are out of place, but rather thanksgiving. For of this you can be sure: No immoral, impure or greedy person—such a man is an idolater—has any inheritance in the kingdom of Christ and of God. (NIV)

As a quick sample, you can see that Paul's comments, taken out of the context in which they were written, can create more questions than they answer. And I'm not alone in this opinion. History demonstrates that the church has battled and divided over application of his words. For example, the proper role of women in the church has been hotly contested among various denominations. In some of Paul's writing, and certainly in the book of Acts, women seem to be seen as equal to men in all aspects of ministry. And yet in his letters Paul seems quite adamant about curtailing the authority of women in the worshipping community. Some denominations ordain women; others do not. Differences in practice illustrate that the interpretation of Scripture is not unified throughout the body of Christ. There are lots of questions to ask. Here are a few:

- Who has authority over our bodies—God, our spouses, or ourselves?
- What does it mean to become "one flesh"?
- Is marriage a co-ownership arrangement or does one partner have more power in the relationship than the other?
- Is marriage a second-rate arrangement with God's first choice being single celibacy for us all?
- Is it really okay to own other people—I mean literally own them?

The answers to these questions partially lie in putting these isolated verses back into their historical context and focusing on what Paul intended to say to his original audience. When that is done, some of the so-called contradictions reconcile themselves. Some don't. It may be as simple as accepting that some terms are used in different ways in different passages. But more discussion is required, and that suits me fine since more discussion among Christians is the goal of this book.

As we pray, ponder, and discuss, we must also acknowledge that we live in another time and culture than did Paul. For example, Paul lived in a society in which some people were viewed as property. Today we do not. We view human beings as individuals with God-given rights. Parents no longer own their children; husbands no longer own their wives; no one legitimately owns slaves.

Because of a difference in our view of property rights, we also define sexual abuse more stringently. No one has the right to violate another's body—not a spouse and most notably not a parent. When a person marries, these basic rights are not discarded. Marriage is seen more as a partnership than as a hierarchy. Most would agree that sexual consent is required by both partners in a marriage. Sex is not something to be demanded or taken from one's spouse.

Our concepts of purity have also altered over time. While I don't personally believe that Paul was anti-body, many have applied his teachings to support that view. Some Christians have been taught that our bodies are dirty, sinful, and shameful. These interpretations are being reexamined, and many corners of Christendom are advancing a more accepting attitude toward our physical selves. A differentiation can be made between our bodies and our proclivity to sin. We are more likely to be encouraged to have healthy body images, to treat ourselves with more respect. You'll hear less talk about sex being "dirty" and more about sex being shared in appropriate and loving relationships.

While Paul's writings have been used by the church to police the marital bedroom in the past, Christendom seems less zealous about such endeavors. Today, few denominations have official statements about specific sexual activities. Some churches still want to control their members. And there is much debate over homosexuality. But at least no one is being burned at the stake. That's a step forward.

Sex, and what Paul has to say about sex, will continue to perplex us. We don't have a consensus on what all these teachings mean. Perhaps it's a positive thing that Paul's writing challenges believers to converse. I have a suspicion that community, rather than consensus, is what God is after.

Chapter 4

Competition for Control of the Early Church

In the early church, three interpretations of Christianity competed for control over the emerging church—the Judaizers, the Gnostics, and (the winner is . . .) Paul and the other writers of the New Testament. If either of the other competing interpretations of Christianity had prevailed, I'm sure history would have played itself out quite differently, and we wouldn't be exploring the issues we are at present. The Scriptures we consider authoritative would not be the ones we revere now; rather Judaistic and Gnostic writings would compose our Scriptures. But the apostolic/Pauline writings prevailed, so we have the Bible with its influence on subsequent happenings.

JUDAIZERS

The Judaizers were Jewish Christians who believed that the only way to God was through Jesus, but that the only way to Jesus was by becoming a Jew. If the Judaizers had had their way, Christians would be following Jewish Law. Observance of the Jewish Law was so ingrained in Judaizers that they could not imagine serving God outside the Law of Moses. Initially, this perspective caused little concern because all of those who converted to Christianity were already circumcised and keeping the Law—Jews and Samaritans. Without a second thought, these new Christians continued to live according to the Law—what other lifestyle would they have?

Friction sparked, however, as evangelistic efforts moved beyond the borders of the Jews into the multicultured world of Gentiles where the Law of Moses was unheard of. Were Gentile converts accountable to the Law? What about eating habits? Could Gentile believers eat what the Jews considered unclean? And what about circumcision? Circumcision, the physical and visible mark on the genitalia of men, historically separated Jews from Gentiles. The Christian controversy over circumcision was, in part, a battle over who had jurisdiction over the bodies of Christian men.

Judaizers insisted that all new converts be circumcised and commit themselves to keeping the Law of the Old Testament. Now, it's one thing to be circumcised when you're a baby boy (although it still seems violating to me), but asking an adult man to be circumcised is a sobering thought. It's also not the best selling point to unbelieving Gentiles. Many males are routinely circumcised in our society, but fortunately, circumcision is not a requirement for church membership.

Scripture tells us that around AD 31 Stephen was martyred by public stoning. To avoid the same fate, many Christians left Jerusalem for Antioch. Some of the Jewish Christians spoke Greek and were more acquainted with non-Jewish cultures. Their faith was communicated to both Jews and Gentiles in Antioch. More and more Gentiles converted to Christianity. Once Paul, a former persecutor of the Christians, literally "saw the light" and turned to Christ, his efforts to bring the gospel to the Gentiles caused the non-Jewish portion of the church to grow exponentially.

The Judaizers didn't like this at all, and their objection wasn't passive. Some of them followed behind Paul, instructing the congregations he had founded to discard Paul's teachings on circumcision and keeping Jewish Law. Their efforts undermined the foundation of the gospel—that we are saved through faith in Christ alone. Of course, this made Paul furious.

Paul and Barnabas squared off with the Judaizers in Antioch around the year AD 50 or 51. Acts 15:1–2 describes how "certain individuals came down from Judea to Antioch and were teaching the believers: 'Unless you are circumcised, according to the custom taught by Moses, you cannot be saved.' This brought Paul and Barnabas into sharp dispute and debate with them" (TNIV).

Paul and Barnabas traveled to Jerusalem to meet with Peter and the other apostles to settle this matter. In a large council meeting, now referred to as the Council of Jerusalem, both sides presented their arguments. After a lot of discussion, Peter stood up and pronounced that God "did not discriminate between us and them [Gentiles], for he purified their hearts by faith. Now then, why do you try to test God by putting on the necks of Gentiles a yoke that neither we nor our ancestors have been able to bear? No! We believe it is through the grace of our Lord Jesus that we are saved, just as they are" (vv. 9–11 TNIV). Had Christians been obligated to the Law, the message of Christ as we know it would have been lost.

Apparently as a sort of consolation prize for the Judaizers, a little "law" was thrown in at the end. Peter concludes with instructions for the Gentiles to "abstain from food polluted by idols, from sexual immorality, from the meat of strangled animals, and from blood" (v. 20). No church that I'm aware of today takes a stand on the first, third, and fourth. Sexual immorality, however, is still a vital topic, and I wouldn't be writing this book if it weren't.

You'd think the matter would have been settled by this proclamation. You'd think that repeatedly telling believers that being saved by faith in Christ alone would have automatically put a lot of issues to rest. You'd think that Jesus's command to love one another would have bridged the gap between Jews and Gentiles. You might even assume, when Jesus told his followers to share bread and wine in remembrance of him, that might have eclipsed the Law of Moses in a Jewish Christian's mind.

But no. Even though Gentiles have their freedom from the Law, some Jewish Christians still felt obligated to follow the Law. Consequently, some of them refused to enter the homes of Gentiles or share meals with them. Obviously this made it hard for the many congregations outside of Jerusalem, which had both Jewish and Gentile members, to come together in home-based worship or to share the Lord's Supper.

After the big council meeting in Jerusalem, Peter visited the church in Antioch. There he worshiped with all of the believers, Jews and Gentiles. He came to the homes of Gentiles and shared meals, including the Lord's Supper, with them.

Then the Judaizers came to town. Knowing how easily they could be upset and hoping to avoid a confrontation, Peter stopped meeting and eating with Gentile believers. This, of course, distressed the Gentiles. Paul arrived on the scene to straighten Peter out in a public confrontation. Poor Peter! He was in the wrong, and now it's written down in the Scriptures so everyone knows. But in his defense, he saw the error of his ways, and as a consequence, more and more Christians realized that every believer—Jew and Gentile—was released from living under obligation to the Law of Moses.

The Judaizers didn't give up and continued to annoy Paul. They continued to interfere with the congregations he had founded, contradicting his teaching and undermining his authority. In several of Paul's letters, he battles the Judaizers doctrinally and defends himself personally. Paul ultimately won the battle. His writings are included in our Scriptures. The writings of Judaizers are not. They continued to plague the church with their teachings through the fifth century. But their concerns still resound in discussions regarding biblical interpretation and Christian ethics.

Some Questions to Consider

1. If we are saved by faith in Christ alone, do we have any relevant relationship to Old Testament Law?
2. Is the Law of Moses a legitimate foundation upon which we can build a Christian ethic?
3. Do we apply the Law literally, contextually, or symbolically?
4. Are we accountable to any religious law at all?
5. What is our current relationship between grace and our behavior?

While the Judaizers are no longer with us, their worries still fret us. How you answer these questions will help shape your Christian ethic and your sexual conduct.

GNOSTIC CHRISTIANS

A second major threat steering the early church in the wrong direction came through a philosophy that permeated the Roman and surrounding cultures—Gnosticism. No one knows for sure where Gnosticism began, but we can be fairly sure that Gnostic ideas were up and running several centuries before Christ was born. At the heart of all Gnostic thought was the concept of dualism—all of existence is divided into two competing parts. There is no gray, only black and white. It should be noted that subgroups abounded within Gnosticism that argued on various aspects of the philosophy. At the risk of oversimplifying, these are some of the basic themes of the dualistic movement:

1. The Spiritual World Is Good, but the Material World Is Bad

There are two worlds and two Gods. The good God, the God of Light, rules over the spiritual realm. The bad God rules over the world in which we live. Everything we can see, feel, touch, smell, taste, hear, or experience in this world is evil.

2. We Are Not Originally from This Bad World; We're from the Good One

Our essence is pure spirituality, and somehow we have gotten trapped in the material world.

3. Our Spiritual Goal Is to Avoid Being Seduced by This World and to Embrace the Spiritual Realm as Much as Possible

We reach our spiritual goal through the "gnosis," or knowledge, that is given to us by the good God. The gnosis reminds us of our original selves and

COMPETITION FOR CONTROL OF THE EARLY CHURCH

directs us toward the Light. This knowledge is a secret that only the Gnostics know and pass on to their cohorts.

When Gnosticism came into contact with Judaism, it adapted easily. The God of the Old Testament was the bad God, who was vengeful and blood-thirsty and who ordered the Jews to slaughter thousands of people in his name. The theme of good versus evil and purity versus impurity fit together nicely. And it took to early Christianity like a duck to water. Gnostic Christians claimed that Jesus was the expression of the good God's love for us. We were engaged in a battle between good and evil, light and darkness.

Wisely, the early church fought Gnosticism with great fervor. Paul warns Timothy to "turn away from godless chatter and the opposing ideas of what is falsely called knowledge" (1 Tim. 6:20). This so-called knowledge denied the core of orthodoxy—that Jesus became fully human and fully divine, was phys-ically born, crucified, and resurrected. Since Gnostic Christians saw the mate-rial world as evil, Jesus couldn't have been a part of that material world. They claimed Jesus was pure spirit. Some said he wasn't actually born—but appeared on the earth as a grown man. Others claimed that Jesus didn't really die on the cross but escaped by trading places with Simon, the man who helped Jesus carry the cross. And he certainly wasn't physically resurrected. The New Testament writers knew that the difference between orthodoxy and Gnosticism wasn't a small technicality. It spoke to the survival of the gospel.

But as hard as the early church fathers fought against Gnostic thought, the allure of dualism was nearly irresistible for some. You can see its influence in some of the interpretations church leaders have made over the years. Dualism seemed to be echoed in scriptural themes such as righteousness versus the flesh, putting on the new man and leaving the old behind, and the spiritual battle against Satan. A fallen humanity can appear to be an evil one. If we look at the New Testament through a Gnostic lens, the heresy can seem more true than false—but false it remains.

In spite of intense efforts on the part of the church to combat Gnosticism, its influence can be seen as Christian thinkers applied dualistic thinking to the faith. Scripture was applied and misapplied in ways that separated the world into the material world containing the body, sexuality, and eventually women in the "bad" category and the spiritual world containing the mind, celibacy, and eventually men in the "good" one. Marriage, elevated by Jesus and the New Testament church, was slowly devalued, and singleness was elevated as a more spiritual lifestyle.

Chapter 5

The Church Fathers Freak Out About Sex

The early church was an underground movement, seen by the majority of Roman culture as a group of atheists who would not bow to Caesar. It was rumored that Christians practiced strange rituals, such as eating flesh and drinking blood. Times of harsh persecution were interspersed with periods of calm and tolerance.

In the fourth century AD, Emperor Constantine gave Christianity official acceptance, bringing significant change to the church. Previously, Christians met in homes led primarily by more informal, usually married leadership. Family life was a common metaphor used in the early church, building on Jesus's teaching about the spiritual redefinition of family and New Testament writers referring to believers as the "children of God." But when the church was legitimized, leadership positions were made more public and political, filled increasingly by those with political power, rather than by selection of a congregation on merit of demonstrated piety and leadership.

Tertullian, one of the church fathers who influenced thinking in the second century, was upset because women were occupying positions of leadership. He presented the church with a new metaphor—a political one. Since women did not hold political office in Roman culture, this shift helped to remove them from leadership. As clerical positions were filled more exclusively with men, and increasingly by bachelors, the church leadership became estranged from real, live women. It's fair to say that too many of the church fathers and others in leadership became obsessed with sex—or rather the absence of sex—through their veneration of celibacy and virginity.

THE MIDDLE AGES BEGIN

The delineation between the early and medieval church eras coincides roughly with the fall of the Roman Empire. The uniting influence of the Roman Empire began to crumble late in the fourth century when Germanic tribes battered through its military boundaries. The empire split in two in AD 410 when the Visigoths plundered Rome. The eastern portion survived as a separate empire, now called the Byzantine Empire, as did the Eastern Orthodox Church, which was under its protection (or persecution as the case may be). The west, in contrast, was in complete disarray.

The plundering of Rome by the Visigoths under King Alaric's command usually marks Europe's transition into the Middle Ages. The Middle Ages lasted around one thousand years, beginning in the early AD 400s and continuing until the Renaissance in the 1400s. Roman law was replaced by chaos as wave after wave of invaders moved throughout Europe, conquering and reconquering the unprotected citizens of small villages, towns, and cities.

Until the 700s, Western Europe was pretty much up for grabs as small military powers battled local rulers. The little semblance of unity binding Western Europe together was maintained by the church through its network of local congregations. Amid cultural and political turbulence, the Western church held on for dear life.

GERMANIC BODY OWNERSHIP

The influx of Germanic tribes brought with it ideas of body ownership, some similar and some differing from Roman law. In regard to marriage, these tribes allowed polygamy, and divorce wasn't all that difficult to arrange. The economic and legal rights of women somewhat expanded under Germanic influence, at times allowing women to agree to marriages on their own behalf. One form of marriage involved a *morgengabe,* or "morning gift." Husbands gave their wives property, theoretically on the morning after consummation. This gift, usually real estate, did not revert back to his family in the event of his death. While he was alive, the husband managed his wife's property but needed her consent in major decisions. As a widow, she could not sell the property if she had children—it being her sons' inheritance.

After some time widows and divorced women, "through no fault of their own," were awarded full control of *morgengabe* obtained through marriage. While there are some differences between Roman and Germanic attitudes toward marriage, there was one element they held in common. Both cultures gave the family the power to arrange marriages without formal governmental or religious involvement.

Feudalism and the Conflict Between Civil and Clerical Power

Property ownership in feudalism took center stage—specifically who could own real estate and make use of it. Feudalism was a system that, in theory, was based on Christian ideals. Paralleling the kingdom of God, with our Lord as King (capital *L*, capital *K*), all land in a particular kingdom belonged to a human lord and king (lowercase *l*, lowercase *k*). The king and all the men the king empowered were called "lords" or "overlords." In a ceremony, the person receiving the land knelt before the king and put his hands in the lord's hands, symbolizing the act of literally putting himself in the hands of the king. The king kissed the person, sometimes referred to as a vassal, and pulled him to his feet. The vassal vowed to serve the king with total loyalty, as a believer would vow to serve Christ. In turn, vassals became overlords and subdivided their lands, offering fiefs to lesser nobles and eventually peasants.

At the top of the social ladder were counts, dukes, barons, and others who had access to the most land. The next rung down was the general category of nobility who were expected to serve as knights in military service. Peasants or serfs were at the bottom. It's not a system most of us would want to live in. But at the time, it served

> > >

> > >

the majority of the population well. It enabled people from all levels of society to gain access to land, and in an agriculturally based economic system, that's really important. Once rights were given to access and work the land, these rights were protected by law and not easily withdrawn. Peasants were able to will their rights to their children, thereby insuring the survival of their families' futures.

But there was a conflict brewing between those who were vowing complete loyalty to Christ and therefore the church but also vowing complete loyalty to their lords and kings. Wouldn't there be a little competition between the clergy and the overlords? Yes indeed! Who would you defer to, the keeper of your soul or the keeper of your livelihood?

And it got even more complicated than that. What if a man was politically powerful and had jurisdiction over land as the overlord and was also ordained as a clergyman? It was possible to be simultaneously a lord and a father. There was no law against clergy becoming landholders and vassals. Loyalty between the overlord and the pope presented clergy with a growing dilemma—it presented overlords and the pope with a colossal power struggle. As they fought it out, the peasants were caught in the crossfire—literally.

Christianity was threatened, not only by the physical violence of Germanic warriors, but by Germanic values

> > >

> > >

and religious beliefs as well. In search of stability, individual believers granted more authority to their congregations and local clergy. In kind, local congregations in the West deferred more and more to the jurisdiction of Rome. The eastern portion of the church, developing a separate identity and history within the Byzantine Empire, was not so motivated to look to Rome as the leader. The more Rome consolidated power over western Christendom, the more the Eastern Orthodox network dug in its heels. With or without support from the East, the church in Rome moved forward to achieve its goal of subduing the impact of Germanic tribes on political and spiritual structures of Western Europe. The Germanic tribes may have been able to trash the Roman Empire, but they were no match for the Roman Catholic Church. Like a glacier, the Catholic church gradually covered the West with its unstoppable power.

A LOT OF FREAKING OUT GOING ON

In AD 107 Ignatius, bishop of Antioch, thought to be a convert of the apostle John, tried to steer the church in a prosexuality direction. Before he was martyred in a Roman amphitheater by being torn to pieces by wild animals, Ignatius cautioned celibate Christians not to see themselves as superior.

But the antisexual bias had already taken root and was growing in support and stamina. The most outspoken and influential church fathers developed theological systems that (1) solidified fathers' and husbands' ownership of daughters and wives, (2) put a new spin on purity by venerating lifelong virginity and celibacy of the clergy, and (3) interfered with marital sex by making specific sexual acts unacceptable and sinful. You can't get any more antisex than that. Here is a brief (there are a lot more, believe me) overview of some of the key rulings of the church in the early and medieval days that relate to property, purity, and practices:

ca. AD 200

Origen, one of the early church fathers, castrated himself. Ouch. He interpreted the saying that "some were called to be eunuchs for the kingdom of God" quite literally.

AD 366

Pope Damascus ruled that it was fine if priests got married—they just couldn't have sex with their wives.

In this same period, St. Ambrose, the bishop of Milan, asserted that virginity was a unique spiritual concept provided by Christianity. He believed that priests should model this ideal and, like Pope Damascus, encouraged married priests to desist from further sexual contact with their wives.

AD 385

Pope Siricius was a busy guy. Even though he was married and had children, he declared it a crime for priests to continue having sex with their wives after ordination. He abandoned his wife and children in order to gain his papal position. Having made such a sacrifice, it isn't surprising that Pope Siricius was adamant about the celibacy of clergy. He supported the idea that Mary was a virgin before, during, and after Jesus's birth.

A thorn in his flesh was a monk named Jovinian who came to Rome and saw marriage as a good thing, talked priests and nuns into marrying, and rejected the extended virginity of Mary. Somewhere around AD 390, Jovinian and some of his followers were brought before a synod, and Pope Siricius had them excommunicated. Unsurprisingly, most of them died early and unpleasant deaths.

ca. AD 393

St. Jerome was as antimarriage, provirgin as they come. He wrote two books asserting that Mary was a virgin before, during, and after giving birth to Christ. The only good thing he could find about marriage was that "it produces virgins."[1] He is also attributed with saying, "If you find things going too well, take a wife."

AD 401

St. Augustine, bishop of Hippo, was one of the two most influential Catholic theologians ever. He wrote that "nothing is so powerful in drawing the spirit of a man downwards as the caresses of a woman."[2] He wrote a lot of other things about sex that we'll discuss in the next section.

AD 401–17

Pope Innocent I increased the power of his station by claiming that he and all the other popes, of course, were successors of the apostolic tradition and therefore as authoritative as the apostle Paul.

AD 445

Pope Leo I didn't, to my knowledge, say anything negative about sex or women. But he expanded papal authority by talking Emperor Valentinian III into enforcing papal decisions through civil power.

AD 494

Pope Gelasius officially forbid women to be in the priesthood. (The implication here, of course, is that prior to this time women were, or wanted to be, members of the clergy.)

AD 826

Theodore of Studius died. He wrote the following antifemale rule for monasteries, forbidding monks to have hens, cows, or female goats: "Have no animal of the female sex in domestic use, seeing that you have renounced the female sex altogether, whether in house or fields, since none of the Holy Fathers had such, nor does nature require them." All right already.

1007

Peter Damian was born. When he grew up, he wrote *Liber Gomorrhianus*, or the Book of Gomorrah, in which he ranked four types of sin "against" nature (all sexual) in ascending order of severity, from masturbation to sodomy.

1074

Pope Gregory VII, made quite a few declarations. First, he decreed that all popes, past and present, were infallible. Second, he demanded that to be ordained, clergy must first pledge celibacy. He also must have felt that the laity in general and women in particular were exercising too much power in the church when he wrote, "The church cannot escape from the clutches of laity unless priests first escape the clutches of their wives."

1089–1090

Pope Urban II and the Synod of Melfi decreed that if a subdeacon was unwilling to leave his wife, it was acceptable for the wife to be enslaved. The trend caught on, and the next year Archbishop Manasse II of Rheims extended this power to the count of Flanders.

1095

Pope Urban II was also a creative fund-raiser. He ordered married priests who ignored celibacy to be imprisoned and their wives and children sold into slavery, and had the proceeds go to the church. He also collected an annual tax, called the *callagium*, allowing clergy to have mistresses. Clergy were fine as long as they didn't marry the women with whom they lived.

1100s

Divorce became a sin, and if you were divorced, you couldn't receive Eucharist. Prior to this time, when marriages were officially dissolved, people retained their standing with the church and were free to remarry.

1139

In an overt effort to bring land and wealth under the church's domain, Pope Innocent II and the Second Lateran Council seized land assets of married priests and demoted their wives to the status of concubines. (Isn't it amazing how anti-family these guys were? They thought nothing of ripping families apart.)

1216

Pope Innocent III promoted the idea that sex, even within marriage, was always sinful, and therefore, all people are defiled through conception.

ca. 1250

Thomas Aquinas (1225–1274) redeemed sex a bit when he taught that sex was sinful only at the moment of orgasm. Rational thought was equated with spirituality. Aquinas did not believe that anyone was rational, and therefore spiritual, at that particular moment.

THEOLOGICAL THEMES AND ELABORATIONS

Property Rights

At the core of property rights is the issue of who controls whom and who controls what. The institutionalized church was driven by the desire to expand its control over people and to amass as much wealth and land as possible. This desire may have been shrouded in theological language, but the behavior of popes, councils, and others in leadership reveals their true motives. Women were seen as competitors with the church for the loyalty of their husbands, especially those men who served as clergy. The church did not like the fact that inheritance rights traditionally passed on a family's holdings to children. Instead, it wanted everyone who joined the clergy, convent, or monastery to make the church the recipient of their inherited wealth. At times in history, priests were allowed to couple with women—to live with them, have sex with them, and have children—as long as the women were not given the status of "wife" and the children were not acknowledged as heirs. The control of property rights directed many of the actions of the medieval church. The institution of marriage, along with women and children, was the victim of this grasp for power.

Purity

The swing from Old Testament Law to medieval Christianity was an extreme one. Men in ancient Israel could have sex with any woman they wanted as long as another man's property rights weren't violated. The medieval church didn't want anyone to have sex with anyone, under any circumstances, and mounted a major assault on sex itself. Purity was redefined as the absence of sex altogether.

The virtue of virginity was based, first of all, on the virginity of Jesus. It is believed by most orthodox Christians that Jesus never married and therefore was never sexually active. This belief has been challenged from time to time, most recently by *The Da Vinci Code* that claims Jesus and Mary of Magdalene were an item and that Mary had Jesus's child after he was crucified. But generally speaking, it is assumed that Jesus was single. If one wanted to be like Jesus, it seemed reasonable to mirror his sex life—or lack thereof. The veneration of virginity began as an amplification of Jesus's own life experience.

Second came the theological ideas relating to the nature in which Jesus was conceived and brought into human existence. Not only was Jesus a virgin; he was also conceived by a virgin. The gospels of Matthew and Luke both describe Jesus's conception as occurring between the Holy Spirit and a young virgin named Mary. Matthew describes it from Joseph's point of view and Luke from Mary's. Angels met with Joseph (in a dream) and Mary (while she was awake) to explain the nature of the pregnancy and to help them both understand how Mary could conceive without having sex with a man. Matthew explains:

> All this took place to fulfill what the Lord had said through the prophet: "The virgin will be with child and will give birth to a son, and they will call him Immanuel"—which means, "God with us."
>
> When Joseph woke up, he did what the angel of the Lord had commanded him and took Mary home as his wife. But he had no union with her until she gave birth to a son. And he gave him the name Jesus. (Matt. 1:22–25)

Where Have All the Medieval Women Gone?

Over time, medieval society gathered its population into one of three categories: nobility, clergy, and peasants. Women could be found in all three of these categories—by being born into or marrying nobility, being born into or marrying a peasant, or by becoming a nun or an anchorite. Regardless of one's place in society, women were limited in their physical movement by constraints of society and the church. Women were under the full authority of the men in their lives.

The old saying "A woman's place is in the home" was interpreted literally. When we think of women today who choose to be homemakers and stay-at-home moms, we don't imagine them literally held captive in their homes. But women in the Middle Ages were not allowed to move about freely in public. They were kept on the farm or in the manor. Even the movement of noble women was limited to prescribed and monitored locations. In addition to keeping women inside their homes, women were discouraged from attending church when having their menstrual periods. Drawing on Old Testament writings, it was asserted that women were made unclean during menstruation. This argument kept women not only out of church services, but out of church leadership as well.

One of virginity's most enthusiastic supporters was St. Ambrose (AD 397), the bishop of Milan, who felt that virginity—the absence of any sexual intimacy throughout one's lifetime—was a virtue for its own sake. He called for priests to model this ideal, encouraging married priests to desist from further sexual contact with their wives.

St. Augustine (AD 354–430), the bishop of Hippo, knew Ambrose and was influenced by his thinking. Augustine became one of the two most influential theologians of the Catholic church (along with Thomas Aquinas). Passionate about the sinfulness of humanity, Augustine justified his theology by using the reproductive ideas of his day. Medical science had yet to discover that women supplied the egg in the conception equation, believing that women were simply incubators. People believed that human life was carried solely by males in their "seed" or sperm.

→ Augustine

Augustine was the son of Patricius and Monica, who were quite opinionated about Augustine's sex life and marital status. Both of his parents wanted him to provide them with legitimate grandchildren, which required a legitimate marriage. You could say that Augustine's father wasn't the best influence on his son when it came to marriage, however, as Patricius had sex with his slaves—something that Monica knew about and apparently went along with. When Augustine came of age, he followed in his father's sexual

> > >

> > >

footsteps, engaging in sexual relations with the family's slaves, although making certain he avoided the ones his father had slept with. Such a thing would be a violation of Old Testament Law and, by golly, this was a family with standards, after all.

Augustine left home to attend school in Carthage, and he took up with a woman with whom he shared a passionate relationship. Augustine later wrote of this time, describing his longing to be loved. "I was loved, and our love came to the bond of consummation: I wore my chain with bliss but with torment too, for I was scourged with the red hot rods of jealousy, with suspicions and fears and tempers and quarrels."

We do not know if this woman was slave or free, but she did not meet Monica's approval. Augustine lived with her from the age of eighteen to twenty-nine, but he never married her. They did, however, have a child together, a son named Adeodatus, whom Augustine loved deeply. Eventually the couple split up, but Augustine retained a relationship with his son. When Augustine converted to Christianity, he and Adeodatus were both baptized on Easter AD 387 by St. Ambrose. Augustine would have been around thirty-three at this time.

After the relationship with Adeodatus's mother ended,

> > >

> > >

Augustine became engaged to a girl who had not yet turned twelve, the legal age for marriage. Augustine felt unable to wait for her to grow up and hooked up with another woman as a concubine. No one knows if Augustine had any other sexual liaisons. He wrote at length about his struggle with sex and his passion for women. Some speculate that he was extremely promiscuous. However, other scholars argue that the depth of Augustine's angst about sexuality does not prove that, after the age of eighteen, he had more than two monogamous relationships. His "sin" might be better described as refusing to marry rather than having a vast number of partners. When Augustine died in AD 430, at the age of seventy-six, he had been celibate for forty-three years.

*From Confessions.

Augustine built his theological system on an inaccurate understanding of physiology. First, Augustine believed that since sperm carried within it human life, it also carried sin. Second, in order to transmit the sinful seed from man to woman, the sinful act of lust-filled, irrational sex was required. If you took the man out of the picture with his sinful seed and lusty passion and had the Holy Spirit provide a sinless seed with no messy sexual hoopla, then you could have a sinless Jesus.

Augustine constructed a nice and tidy theological construct—but one that simply was not true. We now know that both male and female contribute to the creation of life. The idea that Mary could not transmit sin because she didn't have sex with a man in order to conceive Jesus makes little sense when we know she contributed a human egg to the Jesus equation. Our theology must not be based on Augustine's misconceptions about conception.

Another emerging belief about Mary's virginity was that not only was she a virgin when she conceived, but she was a virgin during and after Jesus's birth. If you can believe it, scholars actually argued over whether Mary's hymen remained intact during childbirth. In the late AD 300s, a man named Jovinian opposed this idea, saying that although Mary conceived as a virgin, after giving birth she was physically different. Jovinian also encouraged celibate priests and nuns to marry, believing that marriage was given by God and should not be discouraged. Pope Siricius was aghast at Jovinian's proclamations and admonitions and excommunicated him and eight of his followers in AD 391. Eventually, Emperor Theodosius had him flogged with a lead-tipped whip and exiled. Jovinian suffered greatly for his support of marriage and a more reasonable view of Mary's sex life.

But Jovinian wasn't in charge. Pope Siricius was. The pope insisted that after Jesus's birth, Mary and Joseph never consummated their marriage. Mary was a virgin until death. Any reference to Jesus's brothers or sisters was actually to extended family such as cousins or indicated that Joseph, being older, had children from a previous marriage. Pope Siricius declared, "Jesus would not have chosen birth from a virgin, had he been forced to look upon her as so unrestrained as to let that womb, from which the body of the Lord was fashioned, that hall of the eternal king, be stained by the presence of male seed. Whoever maintains that, maintains the unbelief of the Jews."[3] (In addition to being antisexual, the pope was also a bit of an anti-Semite.)

Concubines

Roman law forbid people from lower classes to marry people from upper classes. If a woman from a lower class became a sexual partner of a man with higher status, she could never become his wife, only his concubine. Slaves were also unable to enter into legal marriages. Consequently, the New Testament and early church could not have insisted that all couples formally marry. In AD 397, the Council of Toledo gave Christian men the right to have a concubine or a wife, but not both. The church affirmed lifelong, monogamous relationships whether couples were officially married or not. The decree of the Council of Toledo also, indirectly, let Christian men know that they were not free to have sex with their slaves without taking them, essentially, as their partners.

Practice

The church's slogan for sexual practice could have been "Don't have sex, but if you do, don't enjoy it." Sex was bad, bad, bad. To minimize the negative impact of sex, married people were carefully instructed on what to do and not do in their bedrooms. Church teaching emphasized that legitimate sex was for one purpose only—to make children. If that wasn't your intent, then sexual intimacy was forbidden. Once pregnancy was accomplished, it was considered scandalous to have sex with one's wife.

When a woman wasn't pregnant, church leaders were especially aghast at the thought of having sex with a woman on her period—so much so that they forbid anyone to engage in the activity. St. Jerome declared, "When a man has intercourse with his wife at this time, the children born from this union are leprous and hydrocephalic; and the corrupted blood causes the plague-ridden bodies of both sexes to be either too small or too large."[4] A few hundred years later, this idea was still going strong. The Archbishop Caesarius of Arles (AD 542) wrote, "Whoever has relations with his wife during her period will have children that are either leprous or epileptic or possessed by the Devil."[5]

Always interfering with the sex lives of married priests, the church began drawing on the Old Testament with instructions for priests to abstain from sex before performing religious rites. Consequently, Catholic priests from the late AD 300s forward began to forgo sexual intimacy the night before they celebrated the Lord's Supper. This wasn't too much of a problem when services were held once a week. Saturday nights weren't that exciting. But this began to pose a problem to marital bliss when Mass was celebrated every day of the week. This underscored the expectation of continual celibacy for married and unmarried alike.

In the thirteenth century, Thomas Aquinas (1225–1274) extended the acceptability for sex as a last resort for overcoming overwhelming sexual desire, as long as both partners engaged in sex first within a sacramental marriage for the purpose to conceive. Sexual activity that did not meet these criteria was mortally sinful.

Sex was limited by when, how much, and how often. Theologian D. S. Bailey summed it up nicely with these words: "A medieval document admonishes Christian married couples to abstain from sexual intercourse on Thursday in honor of the Lord's Supper, Friday to commemorate the crucifixion,

Saturday in honor of the Blessed Virgin Mary, Sunday for the Resurrection, and Monday for the Poor Souls . . ."[6] As Joan H. Timmerman noted by the title of one of her books, these couples could very well have been heard to say, *Thank God, It's Tuesday.*

 Prostitution

It's highly probable that we all agree that prostitution is a bad thing. But believe it or not, the church and noted theologians have not always agreed. In fact, some of our Christian ancestors saw prostitution as having a positive impact on the welfare of society, family, and the church. Perhaps the most famous theologian in support of prostitution was Thomas Aquinas.

Well, maybe he wasn't a supporter of female prostitutes as much as he accepted them as a "necessary evil" as they gave men an outlet for their sexual needs that could not be met by their wives. It's not clear if he also assumed that "celibate" priests would be utilizing their services as well, but I suspect so. I'm not sure prostitutes would appreciate being compared to sewers, and yet that was his metaphor. Sewers, according to Aquinas, were "necessary to guarantee the wholesomeness of palaces." One isn't inclined to discuss one's sewage system, but one knows it is there to keep things clean. Just flush and look the other way.

Sexual conduct of single people came under the authority of the church as well. It was a gradual process, but eventually anyone who wanted to formally minister through the church had to give up any rights to their sexual selves—male or female. First the role of clergy was limited to men, and then only to celibate men. Women who wanted to devote themselves to spiritual pursuits were also expected to forfeit their sexuality. Furthermore, most women who served the church were physically separated from society, being isolated in convents. Some were allowed to minister to laity but under the strictest of guidelines. It's estimated that by the time Martin Luther made his appearance on the scene, as much as 25 percent of Europe's adult population

A sharp young monk arrives at the monastery. He is assigned to help the other monks in copying the old tomes by hand. He notices, however, that they are copying copies, not the original books. So, the young monk goes to the head monk to ask him about this. He points out that if there was an error in the first copy, that error would be reproduced in every subsequent copy.

The head monk says, "We have been doing it this way for centuries, but you make a good point, my son." So the head monk walks down into the cellar with one of the copies to proof it against the original.

Hours later, nobody has seen him. One of the monks goes downstairs to look for him. He hears sobbing coming from the back of the cellar and discovers the old monk leaning over one of the original manuscripts crying.

"What's wrong?"

"The word was *celebrate*," cries the old monk.

had taken a vow of celibacy by becoming priests, monks, or nuns. That's a lot of celibate people.

It could be argued, however, that the clergy were celibate in name only. Too many popes were related to other popes for anyone to be fooled. Concubines and mistresses were aplenty. Apparently priests could keep their women under wraps if their bishops absolved them, a process that usually involved a monetary exchange. In addition to finding ways to circumvent celibacy vows, life in some of the monasteries and convents was quite cushy in comparison to the living conditions of peasants. These institutions accumulated a great deal of property and wealth over the centuries, allowing for a modicum of comfort and ease. But whether they were enjoying the good life or not, their sex lives were not their own. It was only through corruption and payoffs that anyone could have the freedom to make personal choices regarding his or her sexuality.

Chapter 6

Protestant Property, Purity, and Practices

By the time the Middle Ages ended, making way for the Renaissance and the Reformation, the Roman Catholic Church was defending its position at center stage on a number of fronts. An agrarian society was slowly replaced by a monetary economy through manufacturing and trade. Property rights shifted from having access to land and its produce to the selling of skills and products. No longer able to support themselves solely by farming, many peasants abandoned their farms. Towns developed and, within them, guilds fostering the training of artisans and craftsmen. Towns grew into cities, and local leaders diminished in power as loyalty to larger monarchies grew.

Options for women were a bit more plentiful in a city than on the farm. Some women were allowed to work for their husbands and participate in limited aspects of city life. Eventually, people developed a sense of themselves as members of particular nations rather than beneficiaries of a noble's good graces. As the ideas of the Renaissance took root, people began to think for themselves, relying less and less on the church.

The invention of the printing press, perhaps the most powerful change agent in Western society, took away the monopoly that educated clergy had on ideas and theological thought. Average people learned how to read as there was an explosion of printed tracts, booklets, and books. Since the first book to be printed was the Gutenberg Bible, congregants had their first opportunity in hundreds of years to read Scripture and decide for themselves what they believed—about God and about their personal sexual lives. Additionally, people were able to receive current information about a myriad of topics that included reproduction, child rearing, and other sex-related issues. This sent shock waves through the organized church.

MARTIN LUTHER ON SEX

In the 1500s, Martin Luther ferociously squared off with the Roman Catholic Church, thereby initiating the Reformation. Luther challenged Catholic tradition by elevating Scripture as the bottom-line authority, supported by a personal experience with Christ through faith. Luther insisted that we are saved by faith in Christ alone, requiring no intermediary. His message to the common person was extraordinary—you can have a personal relationship with God outside of the organized church. Christians had seen this as an impossibility for hundreds of years. A fresh application of Jesus's teachings turned society upside down.

One of the issues most hotly contested was the Roman Catholic Church's stand on celibacy for the clergy and disdaining married people as second-class Christians. Luther, a Catholic monk with a vow to celibacy, came to believe that there was no biblical basis for imposed chastity. Luther resented the way the church made decisions concerning his body, his sexuality, and his relationships. Luther himself arranged for the marriage of all the nuns in a convent near his home. The last unmarried nun in the convent was a woman named Katharina von Bora. In 1525, Luther married her himself. They had a passionate relationship of many years, raising six children together.

Basing his arguments in Scripture, Luther insisted that marriage was the intended state for men and women. He started with the Genesis accounts of creation—quoting Genesis 2:18: "It is not good for the man to be alone"—and worked his way through the Bible. He believed that sex was enjoyed by Adam and Eve before the Fall, that filling Eden with children was God's original plan, and that Eve's experience with childbirth would have been painless. After the Fall, sex became intrinsically sinful due to lust, but God's design for sexual intimacy was not entirely thwarted. Procreating within marriage redeemed sexual sin. Luther claimed, "God excuses it by His grace because the estate of marriage is His work, and He preserves in and through the sin all the good which He has implanted and blessed in marriage."

Having children was highly esteemed by Luther as illustrated by his declaration:

> In all nature there was no activity more excellent and more admirable than procreation. After the proclamation of the name of God it is the most important activity Adam and Eve in the state of innocence could carry on—as free from sin in doing this as they were in praising God.

The Romantic Side of the Reformation

John Calvin, advocate of marriage, felt conspicuously single as he entered his thirties. In a letter, Calvin wrote about his personal reason for considering marriage:

> I whom you see so opposed to celibacy am not yet married. Whether I shall ever marry I do not know. In any case, if I take a wife it will be in order that, freed from many cares, I can consecrate myself to the Lord.

Ever the romantic, Calvin wrote in another letter:

> I am not of that passionate race of lovers who when once captivated with the external form embrace also the moral defects it may cover. The only beauty which can please me must be that of a woman who is chaste, agreeable, modest, frugal, patient, and affords me some hope that she will be solicitous for my personal health and prosperity.

True to his word, Calvin went about locating a woman that fit his specified criteria and, in 1540, married Idelette de Bure, a widow he had met while pastoring in Strasbourg.

> > >

> > >

Their rather austere beginning led to a genuine love. Two years later, Idelette gave birth to their only child, who died at birth. Idelette was never the same after that. She was an invalid to her death seven years later in 1549. Her death affected Calvin deeply.

Luther was innovative in still another way. He expected fathers to share parenting responsibilities. He encouraged fathers to share in diapering, bathing, and caring for their children. He wrote:

> Whatever the husband has, this the wife has and possesses in its entirety. Their partnership involves not only their means but also children, food, bed, and dwelling; their purposes, too, are the same. The result is that the husband differs from the wife in no other respect than in sex; otherwise the woman is altogether [as] man . . . [I]f the wife is honorable, virtuous, and pious, she shares in all the cares, endeavors, duties, and functions of her husband.

Few things honored God in Luther's mind more than a couple sharing their love, their home, and the parenting of their children. He lived this out himself as a devoted husband and father of six. Before his death, Luther again went against the custom of his day by willing all he had to his wife, Katharina. His children were instructed to follow her direction regarding the family inheritance for the remainder of her life. Luther continues,

I know that Paul commands: "A bishop should be the husband of one wife." And so we drop all these cursed human regulations, which have crept into the Church, causing only the multiplication of great danger, sin, and evil ... Why should my freedom be taken away from by someone else's superstition and ignorance?

They were completely unjustified in forbidding marriage and in burdening the divine state of the priesthood with the demand of continual celibacy. In doing so they have acted like anti-Christian, tyrannical, unholy scoundrels, occasioning all sorts of terrible, ghastly, countless sins against chastity, in which they are caught to this day. Neither we nor they have been given any power to make a female creature out of a male, or a male out of a female, nor did they have the power to separate these, God's creatures, or to forbid people to live together honorably in marriage. That is why we refuse to accept their confounded celibacy, but rather wish that people be free to choose marriage, as God has ordained and established it. For St. Paul's sayings in 1 Timothy 4, it is a teaching of the Devil.

JOHN CALVIN ON SEX

The second most influential Reformer was John Calvin, the theological father of the Puritans, Congregationalists, Presbyterians, a majority of Baptist congregations, and any other group following in the Reformed tradition. Calvin spent his most influential days in Geneva, writing, teaching, preaching, and trying to gain as much control over the city's citizens as possible.

The Protestant movement was under way by the time John Calvin came on the scene, having been born twenty-five years after Luther. He was, perhaps, as rational as Luther was passionate, although both had a proclivity toward using more colorful and politically incorrect language than we afford our theologians today. Luther and Calvin both opposed mandatory celibacy of clergy and promoted marriage as the preferred state for the majority of God's people. In addition, they held at least three more beliefs regarding marriage in common.

The Authority for Faith and Practice Is Scripture, Not Church Tradition

Basing a theological argument on Scripture was Calvin's forte. Like Luther, Calvin saw Scripture, not tradition, as the foundation for sound doctrine and practice. However, Calvin did not interpret every passage literally and saw some of Paul's directives as opinion or common sense rather than authoritative. For example, he did not believe that Paul intended to infer that marriage was a second-rate status when he wrote that it was better for a man not to marry. Paul, Calvin asserted, was merely being practical about the responsibilities of married life.

Marriage Is an Ordinance Rather Than a Sacrament

Calvin believed that Catholic theologians had made two critical errors in interpreting Scripture. One mistake was the result of an error St. Jerome made when he translated the Vulgate, the authoritative Catholic Bible. The term *mystery* was mistranslated as "sacrament" in Ephesians 5:31–32: "For this cause shall a man leave his father and mother, and shall be joined unto his wife, and they two shall be one flesh. This is a great mystery: but I speak concerning Christ and the church" (KJV). And Catholic theologians had further mistaken the focus of that mystery to be Christ and his church rather than marriage between a man and a woman. Protestants and Catholics still disagree on this passage to this day.

Marriage for Calvin was a matter to be arranged by parents, as those of marrying age generally lacked the maturity for making such a significant decision. However, Calvin insisted that no one be forced into an unwanted marriage, and once a woman turned eighteen or a man twenty, he or she could marry with or without parental consent. A marriage wasn't valid unless sexually consummated and could be annulled if one of the parties could not perform sexually. Otherwise, divorce was limited to adultery, extreme incompatibility, or abandonment. The idea of no-fault divorce hadn't yet been conceived. A legitimate divorce required a guilty party. After divorce, only the innocent party could remarry.

The Proper Structure for Marriage and Society Is a Hierarchy, with Men at the Top

As any person influenced by the ideas of his day, Calvin's attitudes about men and women impacted his views. On one hand, Calvin was so convinced of male superiority that he laid the blame for the Fall at Adam's feet, not Eve's, as had the Catholic church. Within marriage, both men and women had equality to conjugal rights. But Eve had been created as Adam's helpmate, not the other way around. Husbands were brought before the courts in cases of domestic violence—a man was not allowed to physically abuse his wife. But he was the head of the house, and she was to submit to his direction. If she resisted, it was paramount to disobeying God.

And yet Calvin also promoted the understanding that both men and women were equal before God. He wrote about Jesus's inclusion of women as followers, pointed out that Jesus first revealed himself to a woman at his resurrection, and rejected the correlation between women and the body and men and the mind.

Marriage Has Two Purposes

Like Luther, Calvin believed marriage had two purposes: to allow couples to have children and to help them avoid sexual sin. Our current idea of marriage that includes sexual pleasure and the joys of supportive companionship had yet to be discovered and described by Christian thinkers, Protestant or Catholic.

SEXUAL IMPLICATIONS OF THE REFORMATION

When Luther and Calvin stood nose to nose with Catholicism, they did not see the full implications of their Reformed teachings. They resurrected the idea that we can individually come to God through faith in Christ. By doing so, they unintentionally started a more subtle revolution. Once people feel that they can communicate directly with God and that their spiritual experience is as valid as anyone else's is, it is hard to convince them that they are someone else's property. The Western world would just have to wait a few more centuries for this to come to fruition.

But in reaction, or perhaps over-reaction, to Roman Catholic teaching, Reformers elevated marriage to the exclusion of a life of celibacy. Whereas Catholic clergy were obligated to be single, Protestant clergy were expected to be married. Women who had devoted themselves to lives as celibate nuns were expected to find themselves husbands. While liberating to some, the dark side

> We have always assumed that Queen Elizabeth I of England never married due to reasons of statecraft, but at the risk of being flippant, perhaps a hygienological interpretation might also be considered, taking into account the sovereign's blackened teeth, her foul breath, and her deeply encrusted facial makeup.

of the Protestant movement eliminated the option for women to gain access to education and other opportunities available in convents. Life in monasteries and convents, a legitimate alternative to those who made that choice, was eliminated for Protestants. Convents and monasteries were closed under Protestant direction. Under the Catholic rubric, women had at least two choices: marriage or the convent. Under Protestantism, women had but one. Body ownership of women and children continued to be placed in the hands of men.

Chapter 7

Is There a New Body Ethic in the New World?

As the Reformation played out, Europe was engaged in religious upheaval and political power struggles. One day a person might be in the majority, sitting pretty; the next day the same person was being persecuted and burned at the stake. One day a person was being appointed to a high office, and the next day that one was getting his or her head chopped off. A person might be safe in one's home today and be fleeing to another country tomorrow. It was an unpredictable and violent time—and this only describes how Christians were treating one another!

Some got fed up with it all and risked starting anew in the New World. Since Catholics and Protestants were both victims of persecution, people from both sides opted for a chance for freedom. Roman Catholics primarily came to the New World through a southern route, through South America and some of the Southern states. In the Northeast, newcomers were primarily Protestant at first.

People who went to the New World can be divided into three major categories: people who came voluntarily as free agents; indentured servants who sold their temporary freedom in exchange for passage to the New World; and slaves, primarily from Africa.

Indentured servants eventually were able to earn back their freedom. But not all of the indentured servants came willingly. Some had been in prison for crimes they had committed. Some were in debtors' prison. They had the choice to stay in prison or come to the New World as indentured servants. I know what I'd have chosen.

Among those who came to the New World unwillingly were men and women from Africa who were brought as slaves. There would be no work-for-freedom possibility for them. While England and Europe forbid the importation of slaves, the colonies were quite accommodating. The number of slaves forced to come to America is staggering. During the American Revolution, half of the population was entrapped in slavery.

Both male and female slaves had no control over their bodies. They were beaten and raped as children and as adults. Parents had no rights to their own

> When Richard Owens sold the contract for his servant Anne Gould to Joseph Wicks, he first "did make use of her body" and infected her with venereal disease. The court, ignoring his sexual crime, found Owens guilty of defrauding Wicks and merely ordered him to provide a new servant.[1]

children, who would also live the rest of their lives in slavery. At their masters' discretion, they could be sold, permanently separated from their children and loved ones.

Women in all three categories—free, servant, and slave—were the property of their fathers or husbands. Indentured servants and slaves, male or female, were owned by their masters. Essentially, the only free agents were men. The ones with significant influence were those who owned property in the New World.

> When female servants got pregnant without their masters' permission, they were subjected to whipping or a fine and had to add a year to her service to make up for time lost in pregnancy and childbirth. In Maryland, after 1658, if a female identified the father of her baby, he may be forced to pay for her lost time, or to marry her if he had promised.[2]

THE PROTESTANT FACTOR

The two most influential Protestant groups that first hit American soil were the Puritans and the Quakers. Both groups believed that a personal relationship with God was possible for every individual. The reading of Scripture was highly valued, so girls as well as boys were taught to read. Motherhood was esteemed, with the responsibility for care and education of the children often given to women. We have a number of documents written by these women, illustrating a high level of literacy in both genders.

> → The mating of human and animals, they feared would produce monstrous offspring. For this reason, colonists insisted on punishing not only the man but also the beast, who might bear such monsters . . . Although executions were rare, sexual observation or experimentation with animals was no doubt widespread in colonial America, as in other agricultural societies.[3]

The Puritans

The Puritan movement, a Protestant offshoot that was heavily influenced by the writings of John Calvin, began in the early 1500s during Queen Elizabeth's reign. The Puritans got their name from their desire to purify the Church of England under Elizabeth's charge. Over the next 150 years, the Puritans struggled with various religious and political powers, coming under severe persecution at times. They were formally tossed out of the Church of England in the mid-1660s.

The Puritans had already started immigrating to the New World by the time the Church of England gave them the boot, having first landed in New England in 1640. Thoroughly Calvinistic, Puritans believed that humanity was utterly depraved at birth, requiring strict discipline to achieve sainthood. In spite of having a negative outlook on humanity as a whole, the Puritans were hopeful that they could create a more perfect community for themselves and their children. They enjoyed the freedom they wanted from the confines of the Church of England. Those who disagreed with them in the New World, however, were not granted the opportunity to express themselves as freely.

Puritan Marriage

The Puritan view on marriage was based on one of their core values—the covenant. A covenant was an agreement freely given between or among parties that obligated those involved to a course of action or relationship. And marriage wasn't a one-sided affair giving men total control over their wives. It was unlawful for men to physically abuse their wives. Men also could not abandon their wives and continue to live within the community. If a marriage became so dysfunctional that it disrupted the community, a woman could divorce her husband with community support. A widow was allowed to retain ownership of the property of her late husband. Marriage was also thought to be the norm for adults. Brides were young. Widows were expected to remarry quickly.

The head of the Puritan household was the father. Part of the wife's covenant was to obey her husband. However, in her husband's absence, a wife was expected to run the household and the farm with an equal level of competence. Children and servants were expected to follow the wife's instructions with the same level of obedience they usually gave the father.

Puritan Women

Puritan women, as well as women residing in other communities in the New World, needed to possess a variety of skills in order to survive: vegetable gardening, soap making, weaving, sewing, and cooking. A wife's role came with its own skill mastery that served as a source for self-confidence and esteem. Puritan women were, as were most women in the New World, given double messages: their skills were necessary for the survival of the family, but as wives they were "helpers" to their husbands. They were to be informed and skillful and were to exercise authority at certain times while at others deferring to their husbands.

Women were allowed to be competent but not loud. Those who persistently refused to play submissive roles could be dealt with harshly. Two such women were Anne Hutchinson, an outspoken Puritan, and Mary Dyer, a Quaker who tried to show the Puritans the errors of their ways. Both Anne and Mary were tolerated as long as the Puritans could manage. But in 1638 Anne and her entire family were thrown out of Massachusetts. They moved to New York. Five years later, they were all killed when Native Americans attacked the settlement. Mary didn't fare much better, although she didn't have to wait for an enemy invasion. After being thrown out of the settlement three times and returning three times, Mary was executed by the Puritans in the late 1650s.

 ## Hannah Hill's Recommendations for Quaker Dress and Conduct, 1726

Dear and Well-beloved Sisters:

A weighty Concern coming upon many ffaithful ffriends at this Meeting, in Relation to divers undue Liberties that are too frequently taken by some . . . Tenderly to Caution & Advise ffriends against those things which we think Inconsistent with our Ancient Christian Testimony of Plainness . . .

As first, That Immodest ffashion of hooped Pettycoats . . .

And also That None of Sd ffriends Accustom themselves to wear their Gowns with Superfluous ffolds behind, but plain and Decent. Nor to go without Aprons . . . Nor to wear their heads drest high . . .

> > >

> > >

And that ffriends are careful to avoid Wearing of Stript Shoos, or Red or White heel'd Shoos . . .

Likewise, That all ffriends be Careful to Avoid Superfluity of Furniture in their Houses . . .

And also that no ffriends Use ye Irreverent practice of taking Snuff, or handing Snuff boxes one to Another in Meetings.

Also that ffriends Avoid ye Unnecessary use of ffans in Meetings . . .

And also That ffriends do not Accustom themselves to go in bare Breasts or bare Necks.

There is Likewise a Tender Concern upon our minds to recommend unto all ffriends, the Constant use of ye plain Language . . .

Dear Sisters, These Things we Solidly recommend . . . That we might be unto ye Lord, a Chosen Generation, A Royal Priesthood, An Holy Nation, A Peculair People . . .

Signed on behalf & by ordr of ye sd
meeting By Hannah Hill[4]

The Quakers

The second religious group of note was the Quakers. The Puritans and the Quakers differed somewhat from each other. You might say the Quaker women were a bit more uppity. Quakers believed that each person possessed an "inner light," could make personal contact with God, and did not need a go-between. Quaker women were given options that most Christian women had not enjoyed up to this time. The movement was lay led, without professional clergy. As a consequence, women could speak up in public, take on ministry roles, and travel while preaching their take on the gospel. Women exercised more power over their choices and their bodies than their Puritan counterparts.

1700s

The reference in the U.S. Constitution to the "pursuit of happiness" was a second draft of language. An earlier version used the phrase "life, liberty, and property," but the framers of the Constitution backed away from that guarantee, settling on a less specific term.

Perhaps it is time to more clearly define what the right to the pursuit of happiness might mean. For example, is there a "right" to a good life? The right to economic security must be at the core of the good life, and it goes without saying that freedom must be part of the good life as well. But there are other, less tangible aspects of the good life to be considered, including such values as living simply through reduced levels of consumption, seeking quality instead of quantity as the measure of satisfaction, and connecting in meaningful ways with others in a sharing and caring community—these also shape the good life and contribute to personal happiness.

> In 1650, young Samuel Terry of Springfield, Massachusetts, distressed his neighbors when, during the Sabbath sermon, he stood outside the meetinghouse "chaf-
>
> > > >

> > >

ing his yard to provoke lust." Several lashes on the back may have dissuaded him, but in 1661 Samuel Terry endured another punishment for sexual misconduct. Not worried, his bride of five months gave birth to their first child, clear evidence that the pair had indulged in premarital intercourse. A four-pound fine was not the last Terry would pay for defying the moral standards of his community.

In 1673 the court fined Terry and eight other men who had performed an "immodest and beastly" play. Despite his history of sexual offenses, however, a sinner like Samuel Terry could command respect among his peers. Terry not only served as a town constable, but, in addition, the court entrusted him with the custody of another man's infant son. In short, as long as he accepted punishment for his transgression, Samuel Terry remained a citizen in good standing.[5]

The Revolutionary War

I am proud to be an American, and I cherish the ideals upon which this country was founded. I look at history and am amazed at how wise and courageous our Founding Fathers were. At the same time, I also recognize that mistakes in judgment were made. For example, it should be remembered that the American Revolution was a war fought by men who owned property for the benefit of men who owned property. When the famous words "all men are created equal" were penned, what was meant was "all men who own property are created equal." Men who did not own property and every woman in the nation, whether she owned property or not, were not created equal.

The exclusion of women and the inclusion of slavery were not oversights. Those who owned their wives, children, and slaves weren't about to give up their property rights voluntarily. These issues were discussed in detail among the founders of our country. They knew full well the implications of their decisions.

John Q. Adams was instrumental in the American Revolution and served as our second president. His wife, Abigail Adams, an intelligent, well-educated woman, laid it out for her husband in a letter she wrote him, saying:

> I desire you would remember the Ladies, and be more gen-
> erous and favorable to them than your ancestors. Do not put
> such unlimited power into the hands of the Husbands.
> Remember all Men would be tyrants if they could. If particular
> care and attention is not paid to the Ladies we are determined
> to foment a Rebellion, and will not hold ourselves bound by any
> Laws in which we have no voice, or Representation.

She couldn't have been clearer. She told her husband that, as his men had fought for their right to a government of representation, they must not simultaneously deprive the majority of people in the country from their right to representation.

John did not take his wife's advice. He wrote her back, stating, "Depend upon it, We know better than to repeal our Masculine systems." And so it was. Just to be sure no one misunderstood who was who in this new country, the year after independence was declared in 1776, all of the states in the Union passed laws prohibiting women to vote.

How much better it would have been if the Founding Fathers had simply stated that all human beings are created equal. That would have eliminated the possibility of one human being having the right to own another human being. And we could have avoided the bloody, costly battles that eventually freed the slaves and gave every adult, male and female, the right to vote. But those events were to happen many years after our nation was initially founded. Drawing primarily from English law, each of the states in the newly established country was allowed to set up its own legal systems, which, of course, included laws concerning marriage and the legal status of women and children.

In England's system a man and his bride became one legal entity upon marrying. They became him. Once married, a woman disappeared on the legal radar screen. Her husband was given full ownership of all her property, real or personal, including all the wages she might earn in the future. A British attorney named Blackstone summed things up in his commentary on English law when he wrote:

> By marriage, the husband and wife are one in law: that is, the very being or legal existence of the woman is suspended during the marriage, or at least is incorporated and consolidated into that of the husband; under whose wing, protection, and cover, she performs every thing.

1800s

The nineteenth century brought about drastic changes in American culture and its legal declarations regarding body ownership. A number of religious movements, here and abroad, a civil war, and plenty of social reform organizations impacted laws concerning property ownership, attitudes toward sexual purity, and even the Constitution. Advocates of various social movements became intertwined with one another, often promoting one another's causes.

Christian Movements

Within the Christian community, there were at least three major influences that directly or indirectly affected women and their roles in church and family:

The Great Awakening

Women were tangentially empowered by movements in different denominations. One such influence was a series of Christian revivals we now call the Great Awakenings that spread through the States, especially in the western regions. The first of the Great Awakenings occurred in the early 1700s and the second in the early 1800s; evangelistic, enthusiastic, and emotional, these revival meetings, or "camp meetings," drew thousands of people. Once again, emphasis was placed on having a personal experience with Jesus, which always poses a threat to the status quo. Women felt more empowered to view their experiences as equal to those of men.

Missionary Efforts

A second empowering influence was the emergence of women's missionary efforts through which women legitimately organized their own associations, published materials, traveled internationally, and learned skills previously unavailable to women. Even though, in general, women were not allowed high positions in church leadership, within their designated roles women gained competence and self-confidence.

Education and Ordination

Even though women were educated and literate, they were barred from seminary and higher educational opportunities during this time. These practices were challenged in the early 1800s. By 1830, women were given the right to college-level education. The demand for educational opportunities was coupled with a growing desire for ordination within Protestant clergy. One of the most significant moments occurred in 1848 when the Seneca Falls Women's Rights Convention, a cross-denominational meeting, unanimously passed a resolution calling for women to be allowed in the pulpit. Such events and happenings impacted particular denominations and spurred the formation of new churches. The church I grew up in, the Church of the Nazarene, was founded in the late 1800s. From the beginning, women were ordained alongside men with full status in church ministry. Other denominations began to open their pulpits to women as well as men. Yet even today, some denominations interpret Paul's writings to indicate that women should not be in church leadership, such as the Southern Baptist Convention, the Roman Catholic Church, and all Eastern Orthodox congregations.

VICTORIAN ERA, 1837–1901

Even though the United States and England had formally parted ways in the late 1700s, the two societies continued to influence each other culturally. Queen Victoria began her long rule in 1837 and had so much influence over Western culture that the entire era now carries her name. The Victorian era concluded with her death in 1901. The queen and the era are remembered by strict moral convictions and clear guidelines for proper conduct between the genders. In medieval society, you may recall, women were feared as sexually dangerous, disdained for lacking self-control, and seen as easily corrupted. Men, in contrast, were sexually vulnerable, self-disciplined, and a needed stabilizing influence. These attitudes were all but reversed during the middle and late 1800s.

In the age of Victoria, women were, by nature, more moral and spiritual yet more emotional than men. Men were rational and levelheaded yet, by nature, the more sexual of the two genders. Women were to assert their pure and loving natures, thereby having a calming effect on the wildness of males. Naturally domesticated, wives were to assist men in settling down and becoming respectable husbands and fathers. It was assumed that men enjoyed sex, while women did not. Queen Victoria instructed her subjects to "think of England" while having sex to keep their minds off its unpleasantness or, God forbid, its pleasure. While women on this side of the Atlantic probably weren't thinking of England, the message that women were not to enjoy sex came through loud and clear.

Abolitionist Movement

The first to speak out against slavery were the Quakers, who let their views be known as early as the 1600s. But it wasn't until 1787 that the Abolition Society was founded. This was quite a challenge for many as it required bucking the social, religious, and economic systems the nation had implemented since its inception. And it brought into consciousness the tension among various Christian principles such as the support for slavery sprinkled throughout Scripture, the sanctity of marriage and family that was denied to slaves, the dignity of each human being in Christ, and the power allocated to men by tradition and Scripture. Christians in the abolitionist movement called not only slavery into question, but a great many other cherished ideals traditionally held by the church as well.

The church was as divided as the country over the issue of slavery—and each side used Scripture and tradition to support its perspective. The Episcopal Church was the only major denomination that didn't split during the Civil War. Those who ended up with one or more denominational splits include Presbyterians, Lutherans, and Methodists.

Both men and women of all racial backgrounds entered into the political fight against slavery. Many of the middle-class white women involved found that in the middle of arguing for the emancipation of slaves, they were arguing for their own emancipation as well. When the Civil War ended and voting rights were given out, a great many of these women hoped to gain the right to vote along with emancipated slaves. Undoubtedly, so did the women freed from slavery. The Fourteenth Amendment, however, fell short of what women of all races were expecting. The issue was clearly settled in 1874 when the Supreme Court officially ruled that the Fourteenth Amendment did not grant women the right to vote. Many women who had worked tirelessly for many years were severely disappointed.

Women's Suffrage

Even though women did not succeed in getting the right to vote in the 1800s, major strides were taken in the expansion of women's rights in this decade. For example, 1839 marks the date when Mississippi lawmakers gave women in their state the right to own property in their own names—as long as they had their husbands' permission. Mississippi was the first state to grant women rights to real estate.

The year 1848 marked two important events that took place for women, as citizens and in terms of property rights. First, a gathering of impassioned women and even a few men gathered at Seneca Falls in New York. Approximately three hundred women (and a few men) called for the end of discrimination against women.

That same year, due to pressure put on various states to expand the property rights of women, the state of New York passed the Married Woman's Property Act. This act allowed married women to own their own property, real and personal—including what they earned working outside the home. They were allowed the freedom to trade, to sue, to be sued, and to be party to a contract without their husbands' formal consent. In addition, women in the state of New York were given equal guardianship of their children and received an equal share with their children of their husbands' holdings in the event of their deaths. This was a huge breakthrough for women.

Unfortunately, twelve years later this act was amended, essentially reversing the rights of married women. In 1860, New York reduced a mother's jurisdiction over her children, but before a father could "bind out or will away" a child, he had to get his wife's consent in writing. All other aspects of the 1848 act were withdrawn. Don't be dismayed, however, because by the turn of the century, most states were headed in the direction of giving women the right to own property and shared parental rights over their children. The country had to go through a civil war and a few other major traumas before appropriating rights to women.

Temperance Movement

Even though one of the first temperance groups organized in the United States was founded in New York in 1808, it wasn't until the latter half of the nineteenth century that the temperance movement really picked up steam in the States and internationally. Two of the most influential groups in the States were the Women's Christian Temperance Union, founded in 1874, and the

→ Susan B. Anthony

Susan followed in her father's reformer footsteps. Daniel Anthony was active in the abolitionist movement, giving her confidence in her beliefs and that things should and could be changed. When she became a teacher at the age of seventeen in New York State, she took on her first cause, advocating coeducation, equal pay for female teachers, and the development of college educational opportunities for women.

Over her lifetime, Susan combined her passion for many social issues, including the abolition of slavery, the prohibition of alcohol, and the extension of property and parental rights of women. She was instrumental in founding a number of organizations that advocated social change. For instance, when women were forbidden to join the Sons of Temperance, Susan responded by setting up her own group, the Daughters of Temperance. In 1863, she was active in the Women's Loyal League that supported Abraham Lincoln's vision of emancipation. Susan cofounded the National Woman Suffrage Association in 1869 and lectured throughout the United States and Europe, advocating the rights of women to vote, own property, and have parental rights to their own children.

Anti-Saloon League, founded more than twenty years later in 1895. Evangelical Protestant churches were quite influential in the movement.

Initially, the temperance movement advocated "temperance" or moderation in alcohol consumption. The focus then shifted to personal abstinence. By the turn of the century, the movement was calling for governmental intervention in the matter, advocating for legal prohibition of alcohol sales nationally.

The temperance movement brought together groups that might otherwise be at odds, such as conservative-minded church groups and advocates of women's rights. Susan B. Anthony, now known more for her impact on women's issues, was a strong supporter of the temperance movement. After decades of pressure put on governmental bodies, the Eighteenth Amendment was passed in 1919 prohibiting the manufacturing, transporting, and selling of alcoholic beverages.

→ Carry Nation

Carry Nation was a force to be reckoned with. Her first marriage, to a doctor who drank too much, began in 1867 and ended badly. Ten years after her first marriage, Carry married a minister named David Nation. She became convinced that God had commissioned her to protest the use of alcohol. Around the turn of the century, she interpreted her divine guidance as a call to literally destroy saloons. At 6 feet and 175 pounds, Carry was hard to stop as she took her hatchet and smashed saloon after saloon into smithereens.

> > >

Unsurprisingly, Carry's attacks were countered with violence, and she was beaten many times in her saloon escapades. She was also arrested nearly thirty times, bringing her sympathetic notoriety. In spite of Carry's enthusiasm, suffrage and temperance organizations were reluctant to associate with her, so Carry had to carry on her campaign on her own. But her efforts added to the fervor that eventually led to prohibition and the right for women to vote.

Antivice Movement

Some of today's more conservative activists may feel comfortable tracing their roots back to the late 1800s, at the beginning of what was then called the Societies of Suppression of Vice. Finding its origin and much of its energy in conservative Protestantism, vice societies found support in denominations, such as the Episcopal Church, the Salvation Army, and Friends Societies. Parachurch and service organizations, such as the Young Men's Christian Association, the Boy Scouts, and a number of state charity groups were among the movement's supporters.

Vice societies saw a connection among activities such as alcohol abuse, crime, prostitution, gambling, and pornography. They opposed the manufacturing and distribution of materials considered sexually explicit, such as playing cards printed with pictures of naked women or nude paintings common to saloons. Along with opposing erotic material, vice societies were often against the distribution of any information regarding sex. This is illustrated by their support of the Comstock Act of 1873, which banned mailing any sexual information using the United States Postal Service, including information about birth control and contraceptives. This law remained in force until 1936. The need to censure activities and materials that were perceived as sexual took an extreme turn when some groups condemned ballet performances and campaigned to cover piano legs.

The antivice movement's accomplishments include opposing the normalization of prostitution in the late 1800s, successfully establishing laws for the age of sexual consent (between 1886 and 1895), and curtailing the "white slavery" underground that entrapped girls, boys, and women in the sex trade.

Alongside these advances, the movement also aggravated racism in its day. The fear about genuine cases of sex slavery was mixed with attitudes that opposed white women being sexually intimate with nonwhite men. White slavery, the movement insisted, was initiated by "foreigners." As a result, southern Europeans, African Americans, Middle Easterners, and Asians became the focus of a number of hate crimes. An example of this attitude reaching into the twentieth century is the charging of Jack Johnson, the first African-American boxing champion, of abducting a white woman. Arrested in 1912, Johnson was eventually sentenced to one year in prison. The woman Johnson supposedly abducted was his wife, who had married him by choice.

1900s

Many of the movements that began in the 1800s were marked with some kind of closure or turning point in the early 1900s. The women's suffrage movement, beginning in Seneca Falls in 1848, culminated with the passage of the Nineteenth Amendment in 1920, finally granting women the right to vote.

The temperance movement's success was intense but short-lived, as it resulted in the passing of the Eighteenth Amendment in 1919 prohibiting the manufacturing, transporting, and selling of alcoholic beverages. The Prohibition Era, as we call it today, lasted for fourteen years, filled with bootlegging, illegal transporting, and the manufacturing of inferior and even lethal drink. The amendment was repealed in 1933. The antivice movement increased the public's awareness of sexual abuse among children and established a consensus regarding an appropriate age of sexual consent. And thanks to the combined efforts of the abolitionist and women's suffrage movements, no one, male or female, was to be owned by another human being. As these ideals worked themselves out legally and socially, women gained more rights to property, especially ownership over their own bodies.

→ Women Owe a Lot to Alice

A Quaker named Alice Paul used her body as a weapon against those who would not grant women the right to vote. She put herself in danger when, in 1917, she and other suffragettes picketed in front of Woodrow Wilson's White House. The signs they carried challenged a national policy that sent U.S. soldiers to fight in a war overseas in the defense of liberty, while American women were denied the same rights here at home.

The police looked the other way when these women were attacked by spectators. But soon the police joined in,

> > >

> > >

arresting them for obstructing traffic. Opposition to the movement escalated until women were sent to jail for various periods of time. Finally, the police recognized that Alice was central to the cause, and she was arrested and sentenced to seven months in prison.

Her treatment was harsh—first solitary confinement and only bread and water for nourishment. Weakened, she was taken to the prison hospital where she realized that she had little control over anything but her own body. So she refused to eat.

This did not make those in charge very happy. To scare her into changing her mind, she was put in the psych ward. While her body became weaker, her will remained strong. Fearing she would die and become a martyr for the suffrage movement, she was force-fed. Three times a day a tube was thrust down her throat through which fluids were poured into her stomach. Her suffering was immeasurable. And when the story was told, the public was horrified at the lengths taken to control Alice Paul. As a consequence, opinion changed and support shifted toward the suffragettes.

Woodrow Wilson succumbed to political pressure, declaring his support for suffrage in January 1918—a year after the picketers began their vigil in front of the White House. By June 1919, the Susan B. Anthony Amendment

> > >

> > >

was passed by both the House and the Senate, granting women the right to vote. The following year, the Nineteenth Amendment was formally ratified. Women owe a lot to Alice, who almost lost her life trying to gain legal owner-ship of her body and equal civil liberties.

In spite of these positive changes, the first half of the century wasn't very pleasant. First, there was World War I from 1914 to 1918, in which at least ten million people were killed and twenty million more wounded. Prohibition, which was good news for some, ushered in an era of organized crime and political corruption. In its midst, the Great Depression hit in 1929 when the stock market crashed. At its worst moments, nearly one-third of the labor market was unemployed. Our financial legs were still faltering beneath us when Hitler led the world into the misery of World War II on September 1, 1939, with the invasion of Poland. While we were looking across the Atlantic and trying to stay out of the fray, the Japanese invaded from the west on December 7, 1941, with the attack on Pearl Harbor. We engaged in war in Europe and the Pacific. Once Hitler was defeated, Americans hoped we'd heard the last bad news from Europe. Then our soldiers marched into German concentration camps and discovered the horrors of ethnic and reli-gious persecution. And the grand finale was a mushroom cloud over two cities in Japan that killed over two hundred thousand Japanese and scared the rest of us to death. One estimate sets the dead from World War II at four-teen million and another five million permanently disabled.

The Second Half of the Twentieth Century

As fascism threatened world peace in the first half of the century, communism emerged as a danger in the second. Unresolved issues in Asia at the end of World War II brought American military to Korea from 1950 through 1953. More than fifty thousand American lives were lost and more than one hundred thousand were wounded in the Korean War. It is estimated that Chinese and Korean casualties were close to five hundred thousand.

As the world changed, so did expectations from and opportunities for women. Initially, women fought for the right to work outside the home. When men were deployed in World War II, women were expected to work to help the war effort in all sorts of jobs previously restricted to men. But when American veterans returned home, women in the 1950s were once again pointed in the direction of domestic life.

With the end of the Korean War, people tried to create happier days by the building of innumerable tract homes, each equipped with a real or imaginary white picket fence. Understandably, Americans wanted a hopeful vision of the future. For mainstream white America, that meant a family comprised of a working dad, a stay-at-home mom, two and one-half children, and a dog, with plenty of room to play in the backyard. For minorities, this ideal was essentially out of reach.

The hope of a tranquil America ended abruptly in 1963 when President John Kennedy was assassinated, thrusting the country into a decade of turmoil. The shared concerns that had brought many Christians together in the 1800s and early 1900s no longer held strong. The suffrage and abolitionist movements veered to the left, and the temperance and antivice movements headed to the right.

A number of forces came together to create "the sixties" phenomenon, including the research of a man named Alfred C. Kinsey. He is often credited with redefining America's view of sexuality, beginning in 1948 when the first copy of *Sexual Behavior in the Human Male* hit the bookstores. His research methodology has since come under serious fire, but at the time, Kinsey's claims rocked our society to its sexual purity core. Five years later, when *Sexual Behavior in the Human Female* was published, the public received Kinsey's revelations with a bit of a yawn. The change in attitude about sexuality had already taken place in the psyche of the nation.

Kinsey presented findings from interviews he did during an eight-year period with 5,300 people. Perhaps the fact that anyone actually admitted to being sexually

> ↓ "It is impossible to estimate the damage this book [*Sexual Behavior in the Human Female*] will do to the already deteriorating morals of America," Billy Graham pronounced in 1953.[6]

active was shocking enough, but the data amazed readers of the 1950s. According to Kinsey, there was a lot more infidelity, masturbating, and homosexual sex going on than had been previously imagined.

Beneath the so-called facts was Kinsey's bias against religious—specifically conservative Christian—sexual values. He believed these attitudes resulted in "repressed" sexual experiences, creating undue guilt and shame. Perhaps his antireligious views, as much as his data, were the trigger for a backlash. But even today, some conservative Christian groups make an effort to discredit his findings and counter the influence Kinsey has had on American sexual morality.

Couple the impact of the Kinsey Report with the creation of the birth control pill, add an unpopular war, and you've got the "sex, drugs, and rock-and-roll" generation. Those who grew up in the sixties were the first to see graphic war scenes on television during the dinner hour. They were also the first generation to reach puberty with a contraceptive that was 99 percent effective in preventing pregnancy. Defiant teens and college students emerged, galvanized in opposition to the war, and dedicated to "free love" and experimental drug use.

→ Margaret Sanger and the Pill

Born in 1883, Margaret Sanger spearheaded a movement to provide sexual information and contraceptives to women, especially those who lived in poverty. In 1915, Margaret was charged with sending information about contraceptives through the mail, and the following year she was arrested for starting a birth control clinic in New York. In 1917, Sanger helped organize the National Birth Control League, which was renamed the American Birth Control League in 1921 and, as of 1942, has been called the Planned Parenthood Federation of America.

Not only did Sanger advocate the distribution of contraceptives, but she also facilitated the creation of the first birth control pill. When it was learned that hormones prevented ovulation in rabbits, Sanger raised $150,000 to pay for research. It took three more decades for "the pill" to be developed for human use, which was introduced to the public in the early 1960s. Sanger continued to advocate for birth control until her death in 1966.

Those following in the footsteps of the suffragettes refocused and eventually referred to themselves as feminists. The good-girl image that Doris Day conveyed in movies of the 1950s was replaced by a sexually free, liberated woman of the '60s. Committed to a woman's right to reproductive privacy and control, the women's movement supported the development and distribution of contraceptives, as well as advocated for the legalization of abortion. Sex discrimination was banned in the workplace in 1964. Women's rights advocates fought for equal pay and reproductive rights (both being property rights issues). In 1966, the National Organization for Women (NOW) was established, an organization that gained in power and popularity during the 1960s and 1970s. In 1972, NOW and other women's rights supporters successfully lobbied for the Equal Rights Amendment (ERA) that passed Congress in 1972. The next year, 1973, the U.S. Supreme Court sanctioned legal access to abortions while giving limited rights to states to intervene in certain cases.

→ ## Are You a Conservative, Liberal, or Moderate?

Just in case you don't know where you stand on the conservative-liberal continuum, here is an easy way to find out. Answer the question: How do I feel about Susan B. Anthony? If you like her, you're probably a liberal or a progressive and may even identify yourself as a feminist. If your blood starts to boil, you're probably a conservative and

> > >

> > >

embrace what many refer to as "family values." (If this book is the first you've heard of her, I urge you to read more history.)

I think if Susan were alive today, she'd be perplexed by our response to her. She wasn't divided over these issues. She actively campaigned against slavery (abolitionist), the abuse of alcohol (member of temperance movement), and pornography, prostitution, and promiscuity (advocate of antivice movement). She fought for women's right to be recognized as full citizens under the law (suffrage). Even though she died in 1906 and was most influential in the nineteenth century, how you feel about her will most likely be influenced by how you view the women's movement of the twentieth century.

Many people believed America was becoming less "moral" due to "liberal" causes, resulting in a strong reaction among Roman Catholics and conservative Protestants. Those who were antifeminist, antiabortion, and for traditional marital roles organized a number of effective networks for policy change. One of the first was an attorney named Phyllis Schlafly, who emerged as a spokeswoman for conservative Christians in 1964 when she wrote her first book, *A Choice Not an Echo*. The book sold three million copies. Due in part (some say largely) to Phyllis's efforts, the ERA failed to be ratified in 1982. Phyllis also spearheaded what is now called Eagle Forum as a "pro-family" organization. Eagle Forum was one of the first pro-life groups advocating the reversal of *Roe v. Wade*.

The Civil-Rights Movement

The horrors of slavery moved a great many people to fight against the ownership of human beings. Consequently, abolitionists were both black and white, male and female. When slavery was abolished and African-American men were granted the right to vote in 1866, many of the white abolitionists saw their job as completed. Unfortunately, the majority of black men were still denied access to the electoral process. No one knows what our country would have been like had Abraham Lincoln lived to implement his reforms, but with his death the federal government made no serious effort to protect the rights, voting or otherwise, of its freed slaves.

By the turn of the century, the focus of many white reformers had turned to other issues. But the black community, often organized around church affiliations, was keenly aware of their situation. In 1909, a group comprised primarily of African-American activists formed the National Negro Committee, which is now the National Association for the Advancement of Colored People (NAACP). Their efforts could not deter Woodrow Wilson from approving segregation in the federal government in 1913. But the president was kind enough to publicly condemn lynching in 1918. Black women, along with women of all racial backgrounds, gained the right

> > >

> > >

to vote in 1920. But this meant very little in practice for African-American women who lived in states determined to keep control of the voting process.

After the Second World War, when middle-class white citizens were experiencing the American dream, African-Americans were trying to get a decent seat on the bus. In 1955, a short, thin black woman named Rosa Parks refused to give up her seat to a white passenger. We now call the brouhaha that resulted the civil-rights movement." Two years later, a clergyman named Martin Luther King Jr. founded the Southern Christian Leadership Conference, dedicated to nonviolent civil disobedience as a means of gaining civil rights for all Americans. It took ten years of struggle before the Voting Rights Act was passed in 1965.

The late 1970s saw the birth of the Moral Majority. Founded by Rev. Jerry Falwell, the Moral Majority advocated for conservative candidates while opposing the ERA, legalized abortion, and homosexual rights. Even though this group formally disbanded in 1989, Rev. Falwell continues to be a symbol of fundamentalist, conservative ideals. Innumerable groups, advocating for and against issues relating to our sexuality, proliferate the Internet as we enter the twenty-first century. Tension over women's rights between progressively and conservatively minded Christians continue today, perhaps more hotly debated than ever.

PROPERTY RIGHTS

The ramifications of personal body ownership impact our understanding of sexuality in many ways. While it is safe to say that most Americans, including Christians, share the belief that each person owns his or her own body, the application of this belief has yet to be fully hammered out. Parental rights have been modified to prohibit the physical and sexual abuse of their children. However, there is still much debate about how much jurisdiction the government should have in the family. It is now legally possible for one spouse to rape the other. And abortion is an issue that divides our church and country.

PURITY

The concept of sexual purity has gone underground in our society today. It is an undercurrent most in a postmodern age do not acknowledge overtly. But in Christian circles, contradictory ideas prevail. On one hand, many aspects of sexuality are seen as "nasty" or "dirty," even though we no longer know why we believe such notions. On the other hand, strong advocates for abstinence until marriage and the "save sex for the one you love" movement actively promote their plans within the church and the larger community. A survey of book titles published by Christian publishers shows a strong movement toward a healthier attitude of sex as sex guides and marriage enrichment for married couples abound. We may not have solid theological legs underneath us, but many Christians intuitively realize that sexuality, created by God, can't be all *that* bad. We want to embrace it, but the church as a whole isn't quite sure how.

PRACTICES

Sex practices are often based on the belief that appropriate sex must take place between two consenting married adults. But the universal church is not united in its pronouncements on specific sexual acts.

- I could not find statements regarding sexual practices such as masturbation, oral sex, or other variations on the theme in any of the denominational Web sites I visited. However, among those who take a stand against homosexuality, there were occasional references to the practice of anal sex or sodomy.
- I was amazed at how many Web sites there are set up by couples who identify themselves as Christian ministries to married couples. I have decided not to list any sites specifically, but there are many that give explicit sexual advice to married couples. In general, most of these ministries promote the idea that most sexual practices are permitted in the marital bedroom as long as both partners consent and feel comfortable with the activity.
- Sex outside of marriage is generally unacceptable, although as we'll see in the discussion of nonmarital sex, the definition of "sex" is unclearly defined.
- Views on sex between same-sex partners divide the church. Those who reject homosexuality do so on at least two grounds: the negative attitude toward the practice of anal sex and the fact that gay and lesbian sex takes place outside of marriage. Supporters of homosexuality claim that the church has no basis on which to regulate the types of sex in which consenting adults engage and argue for allowing gay and lesbian couples to marry.

- Not needing much of a rationale, Christianity has taken a consistent stand against bestiality.

- For a number of reasons, including that children cannot consent, incest and child molestation are forbidden by the church as a whole. The institutionalized church may have trouble effectively responding to child molestation, but all denominations agree that any sort of sexual activity between adults and children is reviled.

- Forced sexual involvement of anyone, regardless of age, is considered to be rape and rejected on spiritual and legal bases.

- Viewing pornography is not considered an appropriate activity, whether a person is married or single. Pornography has become much more accessible through the Internet and has become a problem, most notably, among clergy.

- Abortion is a controversial practice among Christians today. While abortion is not a sexual activity, per se, I've included it because it relates to sex and the possibility of an unwanted pregnancy.

PART 2

Let's Talk Issues

It's finally time to get down to the sexual nitty-gritty. I'd like to start this discussion by complaining about moderates. Moderates are so . . . well, moderate. They tend to see both sides of an issue, or even come up with a third or fourth option. In some of the following debates, the moderates often take up a defendable and reasonable stance. But they don't get worked up enough to set up their own Web sites. They rarely picket when groups they disagree with have conferences. You won't find them forming theological action committees. So it has been hard for me to actually locate moderates. I know you're out there. You're hiding somewhere being reasonable and inconspicuous.

On the other hand, the pro and con sides of these various issues are extremely easy to find. In fact, they're unavoidable. They're in the news. Polarized at either end of the continuum, these folks are always raising a ruckus. But their messages are clear, and I am grateful for that. When appropriate, I will mention sample organizations that support a particular view so that you can follow up if you'd like.

Chapter 8

Sex: Is Sexual Purity a Christian Oxymoron?

S ex . . . is it good? Is it bad? Is sexuality diametrically opposed to Christian spirituality, or can we be sexual and right with God at the same time?

The answer you come to will be shaped by what theological argument you accept (see appendix A: "Deciding How to Decide"). Where a line of thought begins, along with the inevitable assumptions that accompany its beginning, will make a huge difference on the concluding statement. Two of the most influential points of view are based on the theological concept of the incarnation of Christ and original sin. I acknowledge there are other perspectives out there in theology land, but I've decided to limit my discussion to these two because they appear to me as most influential.

INCARNATION OF CHRIST

The Gospel of John tells us that "in the beginning was the Word, and the Word was with God, and the Word was God . . . The Word became flesh and made his dwelling among us. We have seen his glory, the glory of the One and Only, who came from the Father, full of grace and truth" (John 1:1, 14).

God did something quite unexpected and incomprehensible. God became a human being. Jesus, God in the flesh, had a body as you and I do. Jesus got hungry and enjoyed feasting with friends. He got tired and rested. When they beat him, he bled. And when they killed him, he died. He was a flesh-and-blood human being just as we are.

But Jesus was a little different than we are in at least two ways. First, along with being fully human, he was fully divine. That's a little different. And second, Jesus never sinned. That's a lot different. Some people attribute his "never sinning" to his divinity. But I think that's an easy out and, beyond that, not scripturally sound. It's no struggle to believe that since God is perfect it would follow that Jesus was perfect too. Yet Scripture insists that Jesus wasn't different in a way that let him sidestep the genuine and full human experience. He wasn't immune from real temptation. He wasn't protected by his divinity from the depth of human despair we suffer.

Hebrews 4:14–15 reads:

> Therefore, since we have a great high priest who has gone through the heavens, Jesus the Son of God, let us hold firmly to the faith we profess. For we do not have a high priest who is unable to sympathize with our weaknesses, but we have one who has been tempted in every way, just as we are—yet was without sin.

Jesus could have sinned. He didn't. I believe that Jesus showed us that it is possible to be human and sinless—which is a good thing since none of the rest of us has ever or will ever accomplish this feat.

When we take seriously the idea that Jesus was human, fully so, then it makes it harder to desexualize Jesus, something Christians have been doing for a long, long time. It's easier, cleaner, and less distressing to see Jesus as an asexual being, than a real man. Throughout church history, Christians have struggled to hold the divinity and humanity of Christ in tension. But perhaps that is the problem. The nature of Jesus is no balancing act. It's not an "either-or" but a "both-and."

> → God's glory is diminished by any narrowed vision or truncated view of what it means to be a complete embodied person. If embodiment suggests temptation rather than empowerment, if our view of sexuality as a "bodily" characteristic is regarded as something that must be overcome and left unused while mind, will, and other spiritual faculties are to be developed, then our view of sex needs to be reexamined."[1]

I ask the following questions with the utmost respect. They are questions that must be asked, for they are at the heart of this discussion.

• How human do you think Jesus really was?
• Do you think Jesus had an adolescence that was typical of any boy's teenage years?

- Do you think Jesus went through normal adolescent development?
- Did Jesus ever fall in love?
- Did Jesus ever wish he could marry like other men and ask God why it couldn't be?

We know that Jesus prayed in the Garden of Gethsemane to be released from the fate ahead. It seems obvious to us why Jesus would want to avoid the suffering of the death he knew was approaching. But couldn't he also have longed to be released so that he could lead a "normal" life with a woman he loved and a family of his own?

If Jesus wasn't challenged by sexual temptation, then he wasn't really in the game. He didn't really become human—not really. I believe that whatever humanity experiences, Jesus experienced—with one exception. Jesus never responded to any of these challenges, sexual or otherwise, by sinning. We have an undeniable bent to be willful and selfish. Jesus always put God's will first. All the rest of us make decisions that hurt other people and ourselves. He always responded with love. We minimize the suffering of Christ if we take away his sexuality and turn him into an asexual icon. He was a flesh-and-blood man with flesh-and-blood desires. I believe that only when we can embrace Christ as fully sexual yet sinless are we able to find a foundation for our own sexuality and gain a vision of what it could be if sex and love were synonymous.

Anyone who claims to have his or her head around Jesus is either lying or self-deceived. Jesus's teachings and behavior seemed to collide with Jewish culture and Scripture repeatedly. He was always violating some cherished ideal of conduct. Yet he told his listeners, "Do not think that I have come to abolish the Law or the Prophets; I have not come to abolish them but to fulfill them" (Matt. 5:17).

Jesus had a unique way of fulfilling Scripture. He acted in ways that upset people to get their attention and then reinterpreted the law in a way that called for personal accountability. Jesus didn't fit the norm back then. And no matter how much we try to fashion a "Christian" society, or even the church, Jesus doesn't fit in now. He defies our categories. He upsets our systems. He challenges us to love to a degree that makes us uncomfortable. No wonder Jesus got people riled up then. He turned Jewish society on its head. And no wonder Jesus gets people upset today. His teachings are so radical that, as we take them seriously, they will continue to challenge the status quo and our sense of living in a "Christian" society.

ORIGINAL SIN

Genesis tells us that God created man and woman sinless, naked, and unashamed. Humanity subsequently disobeyed God, resulting in an immediate human experience of guilt and shame. Adam and Eve hid themselves from God and from each other, for the first time feeling the need to wear clothes that cover their bodies.

Most churches support the idea of original sin and assert that humanity is fallen. Christians do not agree, however, on what fallenness entails. How we inter-

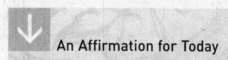

An Affirmation for Today

I assume full responsibility for my actions, except the ones that are someone else's fault.

pret Genesis and apply the concept of original sin to our sex lives makes quite a difference in how we view sex. Here is a brief overview of some of the variations on the theme of original sin:

Sex Was Originally Good Because God Created It

Some people believe that God created sex to be enjoyed by Adam and Eve prior to the Fall. Sex was originally a fully loving experience, pure and ordained by God to be enjoyed by his children. Those who hold this view argue that it was originally possible for human beings to be both sexual and sinless—as sin did not yet exist in the human experience. After the Fall, however, sex was impacted along with all other aspects of our world. It was now possible for sex to be used as a weapon or as a way to distance from other people, rather than for its intended purpose of expressing intimate love.

That's all fine and good, you might be saying. But now humanity is fallen. How does the Fall impact our sexuality? There are a couple of camps who respond as follows:

Sure, Sex Was Originally Good, but Now It's Totally Bad

St. Augustine is one of the most noted advocates of original sin, to which he unabashedly attaches sexual intimacy. In fact, Augustine's theology made people bad even if they didn't have sex. People were conceived via a lustful, sinful sexual moment, so that wickedness was transferred to them from the git-go. A nice example of this mentality was expressed by medieval Pope Innocent III who wrote, "Who could not know that the consummation of marriage never takes place without the flames of lasciviousness, without the pollution of lust, through which the seed that has been received is defiled and destroyed?"[2] Sex requires lust; lust is sinful; therefore we're conceived in sin. Definitely a lose-lose proposition.

Augustine heavily influenced the Catholics from the late 300s on, and John Calvin helped extend this way of thinking to the Protestants in the 1500s forward. According to the idea that we are totally depraved, our intellect, emotions, relationships, and most certainly, our sexuality are intertwined with our sinfulness. Theologically, these Christians believe that God originally created sex as good, but because of the Fall, it is next to impossible to be sexual in a holy way. We are fallen to a significant degree, unable to exercise our free will and utterly dependent on a sovereign God.

Sex Was Originally Good and, in the Right Context, Is Good Today

Although St. Augustine is revered by Eastern Orthodox churches, he didn't have the same impact in the East as he did in the West. His writings, composed in Latin, weren't translated into Greek until the 1300s, at least nine hundred years after he died. Augustine did influence some eastern thinkers, but generally speaking, Augustine and Eastern Orthodox theology do not share the same definition of original sin. For orthodoxy, the term *original sin* indicates the first sin ever committed, the one committed by Adam and Eve. We bear the consequence of their actions by having to live in a world infiltrated by sin. But, for orthodox Christians, we are not sinful because of what Adam and Eve did—we are responsible for our own sinful choices. (For more on orthodox theology, refer to www.oca.org.)

> If any one should say, matrimony is not truly and properly one of the seven sacraments of the Gospel law, instituted by Christ, but an invention of man, not conferring grace, let him be anathema.
>
> —COUNCIL OF TRENT, SESS. XXI, CAN. 1

Additionally, some branches of Protestantism do not share either Augustine's or Calvin's view of original sin. Churches that follow in the footsteps of John Wesley tend to view human beings as retaining the capacity to choose good or evil, a capacity that was damaged but not eliminated by the

Fall. Accordingly, these folks are a bit more likely to see sex as originally good, affected by the Fall, but quite acceptable if experienced within marriage.

God Didn't Create Sex; Adam and Eve Did

A perspective with an extremely negative view of sex asserts that Adam and Eve were not sexual beings prior to the Fall. God didn't create sex; Adam and Eve "ate the fruit" so to speak by having sex with each other. By becoming sexual beings, Adam and Eve disobeyed God and introduced a fallen condition into the world. Sex, for these folks, is essentially sinful. Sex and spirituality are seen as opposites—the more spiritual one is, the less sexual, and vice versa. Sex equals sin; celibacy equals righteousness.

SO WHERE DO YOU STAND?

My bias must be clear by now. As Christians, our point of reference ought to be Jesus; the rest of Scripture, tradition, and experience must square with the person of Christ. As we struggle to understand what the incarnation of God is about, we also struggle with our own sexuality and our ability to be sexual in a vulnerable and giving way.

But a more important concern is where you stand on these issues. Do you see sex being defined primarily in terms of original sin or in relationship to the incarnation of

> The churches need to explicitly teach that sexual pleasure, and bodily pleasure in general, is one important aspect of the individual well-being and therefore of the common good, though its pursuit is always limited by the call to justice, mutuality and neighborly love.[3]
> —CHRISTINE E. GUDORF

Christ? Was sex the sin that Adam and Eve committed, or do you believe that God created sex originally for human beings to share? Must guilt and shame accompany us whenever we are sexual? Or are there contexts in which we can be sinless and sexual as well?

Chapter 9

Nonmarital Sexuality: Can Celibacy Be a Spiritual Discipline?

As a single person, I am very sad to announce that there is not a shred of biblical support or legitimate church tradition that gives any credence to having "righteous" sex outside the context of marriage. I'd been secretly hoping that in the process of doing my research I could find something. But no. If you're not married, you're supposed to be celibate.

However, I don't want to give the impression by this proclamation that single Christians aren't having sex. No siree. Plenty of studies amply demonstrate that Christian singles (at least the ones who are telling the truth) are having just as much sex as the general population. Christian singles just feel guiltier about it.

FOUR TYPES OF SINGLE ADULTS

Don't lump all single Christians into one category, because we can be divided into at least four camps.

1. Pre-married: the teenage to late twenty-somethings who are expecting to marry and just haven't found the right partner yet.
2. Never-married: the early thirty-somethings on up who have yet to get married and are either losing hope or find that the single life is quite satisfying.
3. Divorced singles: those of any age who have gotten married and subsequently divorced. People in this category may have been divorced more than once.
4. Widowed: usually older (but not always) adults who have lost a spouse through death. This group is predominantly female, although men are also included in this category.

The discussion of sexuality varies among these groups. Speaking to a virginal high-school student about abstaining from sex until marriage differs from discussing celibacy among divorced or widowed adults who have experienced full sexual intimacy for an extended period of time. Divorced and widowed people are less likely to just sit on the couch and "pet." The pre-marrieds and never-marrieds are more likely to concern themselves with the question, "Can we do this and still consider ourselves virgins?"

ARE WE HAVING SEX YET?

Scripture does not define what constitutes the act of sex, although it is generally seen as vaginal intercourse. Old and New Testament writers lived in times when sex was equated with marriage, not dating. Under Jewish Law, if a man had sex with a woman, he was either bound to marry her if she was available or be stoned to death for adultery. You didn't get off the hook if you said you only went to "second base" or some other stage of sexual involvement used by singles today. You'd either had sex or not. This distinction was significant since your life could depend on it.

The New Testament church expanded expectations for purity before marriage to include virginity for men as well as women. Both genders were expected to marry young and come to the union with no previous sexual experience. None. Young men had significantly less access to young women than they have today. Unless a young man went to a prostitute, he had very little opportunity to hone his sexual skills. Since daughters were guarded by their fathers as cherished property, no touching was allowed. In essence, if you fondled the merchandise, you were obligated to buy.

We live in a much different society today. So much so, it's hard for us to translate biblical ideas into current practice. We do not demand that couples who hold hands or kiss get married. Old and New Testament cultures did. We date and arrange our own marriages. They didn't. Marriages were arranged by fathers and families. We have extended engagements. Once a couple was betrothed, the wedding followed shortly with minimal prior contact between prospective bride and groom. They didn't have the time or opportunity to get into trouble. We have plenty of both.

As it was for those those living in biblical times, virginity is still valued. But it is much harder for us to define virginity than it was for our spiritual ancestors. In the past, virgins were defined as those who had not experienced vaginal intercourse. But because of the lack of legitimate access, it was also assumed that they had not engaged in any other level of sexual activity either. Today, we still hold on to the idea that virginity is determined by the same standard. But

→ If you are sexually active, especially in a noncommitted, and not fully monogamous relationship, you run the chance of picking up one or more of the following:

Chlamydia, the most commonly reported bacterial STD in the United States, is transmitted during any type of sex. Three-fourths of the three million infections each year occur in people under the age of twenty-five. Many are not aware they are infected because there can be no symptoms until serious irreversible damage has occurred—including infertility. If a woman is pregnant, this disease can also be transmitted to her unborn baby.

Herpes is a disease that can stay in your body indefinitely. Rarely do you have any indication that you have been infected by either type 1 or type 2 of the herpes simplex viruses. Type 1 is spread by coming into contact with an infected person's saliva, resulting in what we often call "fever blisters." Type 2 results in blisters appearing around genitals or rectum. As the blisters break, sores are left that usually take two to four weeks to heal. Outbreaks usually continue at different intervals—weeks or months. These outbreaks can lessen in number and level of discomfort as time goes on.

Gonorrhea is spread through any sexual contact that includes the transmission of bodily fluids. The bacteria grows most quickly in warm, moist areas of the body, including the

> > >

> > >

mouth and throat. The disease can even spread into one's eyes if a person touches his or her eyes after sexual activity. This disease can cause damage to interior sexual organs and be transmitted to the unborn.

Syphilis is passed through direct contact with syphilitic sores that occur primarily on the genitals or anus or on the lips and in the mouth. The disease is spread between sexual partners and can be transmitted to the unborn. It is important to get treatment as soon as possible. Syphilis has three stages; the last can result in serious organ damage including brain damage.

HIV/AIDS is probably the most feared sexually transmitted disease because it is presently incurable and can lead to a premature death. A person's immune system is compromised, which may open the door to other diseases, some that can prove fatal. HIV can be transmitted through any transfer of bodily fluids. A blood test is required to ascertain if a person has been infected. Those with the virus are considered HIV positive.

It is important to be aware that birth control methods such as the pill or the IUD do not protect a woman from being infected by any of these diseases. Depending on the method of transmission, condoms may help prevent diseases transmitted through sex. However, the use of condoms does not protect a person from the oral transmission of an STD.

there is no clear statement regarding the variety of forms of sexual activity other than intercourse.

Applying the vaginal intercourse definition of virginity allows single Christians to engage in a variety of sexual practices and still consider themselves to be virgins. Here are some "not really sex" activities that single Christians have been known to share that can result in pregnancy or the spread of sexually transmitted diseases:

- *Manual stimulation or mutual masturbation:* This activity can result in the passing of sexually transmitted diseases as sexual fluids are manually shared between partners. It is even possible for pregnancy to result if semen is inadvertently transferred to the vaginal area. Sperm don't care how they get into the vaginal fluid and are quite capable of swimming upstream.
- *Oral sex:* Oral sex is not solid protection against HIV and other sexually transmitted diseases. STDs can be transmitted through cuts and sores in one's mouth, some resulting from the activity of oral sex itself. However, it is unlikely a person will end up pregnant engaging in this behavior.
- *Fooling around with clothing on:* As long as there is an exchange of bodily fluids through kissing and touching, it doesn't matter if a couple have kept items of clothing in place. Condoms aren't made out of cloth, after all.

HAVE YOU BEEN UNFAITHFUL TO ME?

We live under a distinct double standard for sexual behavior—one for those outside monogamous relationships and one for those who are part of a couple. If we address this issue from the standpoint of monogamous couples, sexual activity takes on a different connotation. I know of few married or single adults in committed relationships who would view their partners as faithful if they engaged in "anything but" vaginal sex. A more accurate meaning of sexual behavior is reached, with a more realistic understanding of the significance of sexual intimacy, when we contextualize sex within monogamy.

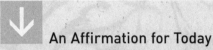

An Affirmation for Today

Good judgment comes from bad experience, and a lot of that comes from bad judgment.

I'd like to suggest a definition of virginity that cuts to the spirit, not the letter, of this issue. A virgin is someone who retains a naiveté in regard to sexual experience. I believe that any activity involving genitalia, especially when it culminates in orgasm, can be defined as sexual. Of course I realize that there may be a lot of "virgins" out there who disagree with me, and you're most welcome to do so.

At the same time, I do not endorse the idea that those who have yet to engage in sex should be sexually illiterate. We all need accurate information about physiology, reproduction, birth control methods, sexually transmitted diseases, and the relational impact of sexual involvement. I do not adhere to the idea that if

> A virgin is someone who retains a naiveté in regard to sexual experience.

you keep people (especially young ones) in the dark about sex, they won't participate. What you don't know can hurt a great deal. If one of our goals as Christians is to learn how to express our sexuality in a responsible manner, we need to understand both sexuality and responsibility. Not just the latter. On this point, concerned parents may disagree with me.

The flip side of sexual involvement is, of course, sexual abstinence. Many parents and other concerned adults are actively involved with the abstinence movement, trying to persuade their children to maintain their sexual naiveté as long as possible. I looked up *abstinence* on the Web, and every site that came up related to teens or college-age people. It didn't matter if the site was sponsored by Christian or secular groups. *Abstinence* is a young person's term. Many of the sites I visited emphasized the many dangers of having sex outside of marriage—such as a broken heart if the relationship breaks up, unwanted pregnancy, and the spread of sexually transmitted diseases. All of these cautions are accurate. But in addition to pointing out the reasons to avoid sex, I'd like to focus on presenting celibacy as a lifestyle to embrace as long as one is single. Rather than trying to be as sexual as possible without crossing the line, the church must be challenged to draw unmarried adults toward celibacy as a spiritual discipline, a state in which God can transform individuals in unique ways.

CELIBACY AS A SPIRITUAL DISCIPLINE

Single adults of any age will be best served when their celibate years are experienced as part of spiritual, emotional, and relational growth, rather than a time of going without. It's easy for never-married, divorced, and widowed Christians to feel as though they're missing out on life. A look around at your average church will reveal that most are comprised of married couples with families. Only a few have ministries to single adults, and a good many of those are waning in numbers and support.

Perhaps the lack of enthusiasm on the part of single adults stems from the definition of celibacy itself. It is the absence of sexual intimacy in one's life. It is a void. Even an emptiness. Who wants to embrace an empty space? As a person who has never married, I feel utterly qualified to challenge the church to develop a view of celibacy that has spiritual depth and content, rather than telling us our "time" will come and we should simply wait. Defining one's life by "not having sex" lacks the focus and motivation needed to live a meaningful spiritual and emotional existence.

Some denominations are well acquainted with the practice of spiritual disciplines. Others have never heard the term. A spiritual discipline, such as prayer, Scripture study, fasting, or reflection, is a practice that is consistently incorporated into one's lifestyle. The purpose is to deepen one's relationship with God as well as to personally grow in character and self-control. Approaching celibacy as a spiritual discipline gives single people focus, purpose, and a way to utilize celibacy in a meaningful way.

One of the major benefits of practicing celibacy as a spiritual discipline is learning how to resist becoming sexually involved with people outside the boundaries of marriage. Self-control is a discipline that is needed whether a person is single or married. As any married person can attest, having a spouse does not eliminate attraction to others. If a person has learned to be sexually chaste when single, he or she will be better equipped to deal with sexual temptation once married.

> Chastity is something you do; it is something you practice. It is not only a state—the state of being *chaste*—but a disciplined, active undertaking that we do as part of the Body. It is not the mere absence of sex but an active conforming of one's body to the arc of the gospel.[1]
>
> —LAUREN F. WINNER

This perspective is gaining popularity among churches. If you are a single adult, I highly recommend transforming your experience into a meaningful journey with God, rather than simply a waiting period of deprivation.

Chapter 10

Abortion: Is This a Body-Ownership Debate?

Most of us believe that every human being, male or female, has the right to body ownership. Pro-choice advocates are profoundly aware of our past. It was not long ago that women had no claim over their own bodies, being the property of fathers and husbands. Yet many women today seem to have completely forgotten about how difficult it has been for us to gain body ownership. Women must not take our current status for granted, as if women's bodies have always been under our personal jurisdiction. Those advocating for pro-choice dig their feet into the soil of the past, fearful that women will lose control over their bodies once again. You can feel the fear. It's palpable.

In their minds, the right to an abortion is equivalent to having body ownership—they are one and the same. A woman, so they argue, has the right to decide if she will make the physical, emotional, and economic sacrifices a pregnancy and birth require. She may decide to raise her child or opt for adoption, but the pregnancy itself is demanding and should not be forced on a woman. If she cannot make the basic decision of whether or not she will give birth, then pro-choice advocates believe we fool ourselves by thinking women truly own their bodies.

Some pro-choice advocates are terrified that if abortion is regulated in any way, we will be plunged back into a time of oppression in which what happens to us will be decided by the government, the church, or some other institution. God has given us the right to control our own bodies, they argue. We must do everything we can to protect this right. This trepidation puts some pro-choice advocates into the position of fighting not simply for the right to choose, but also for the right to partial-birth abortion. I have observed that many who support a woman's right to an abortion early in her pregnancy are equally squeamish about abortion in the last trimester.

On the other side of the issue, you'll find pro-lifers. At the moment of conception, their argument goes, a human being is created. Since all human beings have the right to body ownership, they believe that the unborn has a right to his or her body as well. And the rights of the unborn trump the rights of the pregnant woman.

Since pro-choice advocates also believe that human beings have the right to body ownership, they cannot allow the unborn to be considered fully human. The two sides spin off into medical and theological debates concerning when life begins—at conception, when the first breath is taken, or somewhere in between. Unfortunately, science cannot answer this question for us. In fact, technological breakthroughs seem to only complicate our discussion as in vitro fertilization, artificial insemination, and other fertility measures are developed.

WHERE THE CHURCH STANDS TODAY

A helpful conversation cannot occur in the church when some Christians claim there is nothing to talk about—either God is against abortion and that's the end of the discussion or God supports justice for women and that's the end of the discussion. Those on either extreme are very reluctant to acknowledge that a conversation is necessary. But, in fact, committed Christians are on both sides of this issue. Many fall somewhere in between. Some are confused and don't know what to believe. Let's look at the spectrum of stances churches have made on this issue.

Pro-Life Churches

On the pro-life side are those denominations or conventions that oppose abortion: some oppose it in all instances, while some allow it when necessary to save a woman's life or if the pregnancy is the result of incest or rape.

- African Methodist Episcopal Church
- Assemblies of God
- Church of God in Christ
- Church of the Nazarene
- Eastern Orthodox churches
- Lutheran Church, Missouri Synod
- Progressive National Baptist Convention
- Salvation Army
- Southern Baptist Convention

The following samples are of official statements made by denominations on their Web sites or in other publications:

The Assemblies of God

The Assemblies of God is unashamedly pro-life. Even though a United States Supreme Court decision legalized abortion in 1973, abortion is still immoral and sinful. This stand is founded on the biblical truth that all human life is created in the image of God (Gen. 1:27). From that truth issues the long-standing Christian view that aborting the life of a developing child is evil.

Those who defend abortion claim that an unborn child in the early stages of development is merely fetal tissue, not a person. But neither science nor medicine can declare an arbitrary time during pregnancy when human life begins. The Bible indicates that human life begins at conception (Job 31:15; Ps. 139:13–16). Because of the sacredness of human life, the matter is settled by theological statement of Scripture, not by a medical determination of viability outside the mother's womb.

There is a Christian alternative to abortion. Instead of terminating the life of the unborn child, the newborn can be placed for adoption by loving Christians. Adoption is a concept authored by God, for all Christian believers have been adopted into the family of God. By choosing to give birth to her baby rather than having an abortion, the birth mother spares the life of a child created in the image of God.[1]

Eastern Orthodox Churches

As to abortion, the Church very clearly and absolutely condemns it as an act of murder in every case. If a woman is with child, she must allow it to be born. In regard to all of the very difficult cases, such as a young girl being raped or a mother who is certain to die, the consensus of Orthodox opinion would be that a decision for abortion might possibly be made, but that it can in no way be easily justified as morally righteous, and that persons making such a decision must repent of it and count on the mercy of God. It must be very clear as well that abortion employed for human comfort or to stop what a contraceptive method failed to prevent, is strictly considered by the Canon laws of the Church to be a crime equal to murder.[2]

The Lutheran Church, Missouri Synod

Our church's explanation of the Small Catechism puts the matter well when it says, "The living but unborn are persons in the sight of God from the time of conception. Since abortion takes a human life, it is not a moral option except to prevent the death of another person, the mother." The sin of willfully aborting a child, except in those very rare situations where it may be necessary to save the life of the mother, is a sinful act, totally contrary to the will of God.

If abortion is legal in the United States, how can the church oppose it? Just because something happens to be legal does not make it moral, ethical, or right. Abortion is perhaps one of the most dramatic examples of a situation where something is legal, but is very much a sin against God. Since 1973, abortions have been legal in the United States. Abortion remains a sin against God, whether or not it is legal in our society; therefore we must "obey God rather than men" (Acts 5:29). The church needs to inform its members that abortion is sinful and then encourage them as Christian citizens, to use available legal means to change the law. Christians do not resort to illegal activities to change our nation's laws.[3]

The Salvation Army

The Salvation Army believes in the sanctity of all human life and considers each person to be of infinite value and each life a gift from God to be cherished, nurtured, and redeemed. Human life is sacred because it is made in the image of God and has an eternal destiny (Gen. 1:27). Sacredness is not conferred, nor can it be taken away by human agreement.

The Salvation Army deplores society's ready acceptance of abortion, which reflects insufficient concern for vulnerable persons, including the unborn (Ps. 82:3–4).

The Salvation Army holds to the Christian ideals of chastity before marriage and fidelity within the marriage relationship and, consistent with these ideals, supports measures to prevent crisis pregnancies. It is opposed to abortion as a means of birth control, family planning, sex selection, or for any reason of mere convenience to avoid the responsibility for conception. Therefore, when an unwanted pregnancy occurs, The Salvation Army advises that the situation be accepted and that the pregnancy be carried to term and offers supportive help and assistance with planning.

The Salvation Army recognizes tragic and perplexing circumstances that require difficult decisions regarding a pregnancy. Such decisions should be made only after prayerful and thoughtful consideration, with appropriate involvement of the woman's family and pastoral, medical, and other counsel. A woman in these circumstances needs acceptance, love, and compassion.

When an abortion has taken place, The Salvation Army will continue to show love and compassion and to offer its services and fellowship to those involved.[4]

Southern Baptist Convention

Procreation is a gift from God, a precious trust reserved for marriage. At the moment of conception, a new being enters the universe, a human being, a being created in God's image. This human being deserves our protection, whatever the circumstances of conception.[5]

Pro-Choice

Taking a decidedly pro-choice stance are the following denominations and religiously affiliated groups:

- American Baptist Churches—USA
- American Friends (Quaker) Service Committee
- Catholics for Free Choice
- Christian Church (Disciples of Christ)
- Episcopal Church (USA)
- Episcopal Women's Caucus
- Evangelicals for Choice
- Lutheran Women's Caucus
- Moravian Church in America–Northern Province
- Presbyterian Church (USA)
- Religious Coalition for Reproductive Choice
- United Church of Christ
- United Methodist Church
- Women's Caucus Church of the Brethren

Some pro-choice denominations and groups also post their positional statements on the Web. Here is a small sampling:

Episcopal Church

While we acknowledge that in this country it is the legal right of every woman to have a medically safe abortion, as Christians we believe strongly that if this right is exercised, it should be used only in extreme situations. We emphatically oppose abortion as a means of birth control, family planning, sex selection, or any reason of mere convenience.

In those cases where an abortion is being considered, members of this Church are urged to seek the dictates of their conscience in prayer, to seek the advice and counsel of members of the Christian community and where appropriate, the sacramental life of this Church.

Whenever members of this Church are consulted with regard to a problem pregnancy, they are to explore, with grave seriousness, with the person or persons seeking advice and counsel, as alternatives to abortion, other positive courses of action, including, but not limited to, the following possibilities: the parents raising the child; another family member raising the child; making the child available for adoption.

It is the responsibility of members of this Church, especially the clergy, to become aware of local agencies and resources which will assist those faced with problem pregnancies.

We believe that legislation concerning abortions will not address the root of the problem. We therefore express our deep conviction that any proposed legislation on the part of national or state governments regarding abortions must take special care to see that the individual conscience is respected, and that the responsibility of individuals to reach informed decisions in this matter is acknowledged and honored as the position of this Church; and be it further Resolved, That this 71st General Convention of the Episcopal Church express its unequivocal opposition to any legislative, executive or judicial action on the part of local, state or national governments that abridges the right of a woman to reach an informed decision about the termination of pregnancy or that would limit the access of a woman to safe means of acting on her decision.[6]

Evangelical Lutheran Church in America

The Churchwide Assembly of the Evangelical Lutheran Church in America adopted a statement on abortion in 1991. The following are excerpts from their statement:

Induced abortion, the act of intentionally terminating a developing life in the womb, is one of the issues about which members of the Evangelical Lutheran Church in America have serious differences. These differences are also found within society.

Differences hold promise or peril. Our differences are deep and potentially divisive. However, they are also a gift that can lead us into constructive conversation about our faith and its implications for our life in the world.

A developing life in the womb does not have an absolute right to be born, nor does a pregnant woman have an absolute right to terminate a pregnancy. The concern for both the life of the woman and the developing life in her womb expresses a common commitment to life. This requires that we move beyond the usual "pro-life" versus "pro-choice" language in discussing abortion.

Abortion ought to be an option only of last resort. Therefore, as a church we seek to reduce the need to turn to abortion as the answer to unintended pregnancies.

Because of the Christian presumption to preserve and protect life, this church, in most circumstances, encourages women with unintended pregnancies to continue the pregnancy.

This church encourages and seeks to support adoption as a positive option to abortion.

This church recognizes that there can be sound reasons for ending a pregnancy through induced abortion.

This church opposes ending intrauterine life when a fetus is developed enough to live outside a uterus with the aid of reasonable and necessary technology. If a pregnancy needs to be interrupted after this point, every reasonable and necessary effort should be made to support this life, unless there are lethal fetal abnormalities indicating that the prospective newborn will die very soon.[7]

The United Church of Christ

God has given us life, and life is sacred and good. God has also given us the responsibility to make decisions which reflect a reverence for life in circumstances when conflicting realities are present. Jesus affirmed women as full partners in the faith, capable of making decisions that affect their lives.

If the full range of options available to women concerning reproductive health are compromised, then women's moral agency and ability to make decisions consistent with their faith are compromised. Furthermore, poor women should have equal access to full reproductive health services, including abortion and information on family planning.

The United Church of Christ has affirmed and reaffirmed since 1971 that access to safe and legal abortion is consistent with a woman's right to follow the dictates of her own faith and beliefs in determining when and if she should have children, and has supported comprehensive sexuality education as one measure to prevent unwanted or unplanned pregnancies.[8]

The United Methodist Church

The beginning of life and the ending of life are the God-given boundaries of human existence. While individuals have always had some degree of control over when they would die, they now have the awesome power to determine when and even whether new individuals will be born.

Our belief in the sanctity of unborn human life makes us reluctant to approve abortion. But we are equally bound to respect the sacredness of the life and well-being of the mother, for whom devastating damage may result from an unacceptable pregnancy. In continuity with past Christian teaching, we recognize tragic conflicts of life with life that may justify abortion, and in such cases we support the legal option of abortion under proper medical procedures. We cannot affirm abortion as an acceptable means of birth control, and we unconditionally reject it as a means of gender selection.

We oppose the use of late-term abortion known as dilation and extraction (partial-birth abortion) and call for the end of this practice except when the physical life of the mother is in danger and no other medical procedure is available, or in the case of severe fetal anomalies incompatible with life. We call all Christians to a searching and prayerful inquiry into the sorts of conditions that may warrant abortion. We commit our Church to continue to provide nurturing ministries to those who terminate a pregnancy, to those in the midst of a crisis pregnancy, and to those who give birth.

Governmental laws and regulations do not provide all the guidance required by the informed Christian conscience. Therefore, a decision concerning abortion should be made only after thoughtful and prayerful consideration by the parties involved, with medical, pastoral, and other appropriate counsel.[9]

PARTIAL-BIRTH ABORTION AND POLITICS

The use of partial-birth abortion is offensive to many. And yet a total ban on abortion, forbidding this option for every woman under every circumstance fails to gather as much support as pro-life activists might like. In the middle are groups that support a limited use of abortion, usually taking a stand against late-term abortions.

Among both the pro-choice and pro-life denominations are those that do more than make a statement of belief. They have engaged in activist efforts to either protect *Roe v. Wade* or to repeal a woman's legal rights to abortion. The more political this disagreement becomes, the more divided and antagonistic portions of the church become to each other.

ABORTION IN THE OLD AND NEW TESTAMENT

There is only one verse in the Old and New Testaments that might relate to abortion, although it is argued that this passage deals more with violence against women than it does the status of an unborn child. In Exodus 21:22–23 we read:

> If men strive, and hurt a woman with child, so that her fruit depart from her, and yet no mischief follow: he shall be surely punished, according as the woman's husband will lay upon him, and he shall pay as the judges determine. And if any mischief follow, then thou shalt give life for life. (KJV)

> If people are fighting and a pregnant woman is hit and gives birth prematurely but there is no serious injury, the offender must be fined whatever the woman's husband demands and the court allows. But if there is serious injury, you are to take life for life. (NIV)

Proponents from both sides utilize this verse to support their positions. Pro-lifers often interpret this to mean if a pregnant woman is struck and the woman miscarries but she and the baby are fine, there will be a fine imposed on the man who hit her. If the woman or her baby dies, regardless of the length of pregnancy, the man who hit her will lose his life.

Pro-choicers reject this interpretation, arguing that the verse means if a pregnant woman is struck and the woman miscarries and loses the baby but she survives, there will be a fine imposed on the man who hit her. But if she dies as a consequence, the assailant will lose his life.

So now what do we do?

Additional Scriptures are referred to by both sides as speaking to the unborn. It's important to remember that even though abortion was a practice used in the time of Jesus and at the inception of the church, neither Jesus nor any of the New Testament writers addressed abortion one way or the other. One must infer meaning from other passages to support either side of this issue.

One of the most often quoted verses in this debate is Psalm 139:13–16:

> For you created my inmost being
>> you knit me together in my mother's womb.
> I praise you because I am fearfully and wonderfully made;
>> your works are wonderful,
>> I know that full well.
> My frame was not hidden from you
>> when I was made in the secret place.
> When I was woven together in the depths of the earth,
>> your eyes saw my unformed body.

All the days ordained for me
    were written in your book
    before one of them came to be.

Pro-life supporters interpret this passage to indicate that since God knew us in the womb, human life begins at conception. It is murder to interrupt God as we are knit together in our mothers' wombs.

Pro-choicers, of course, disagree. They argue that this verse reiterates what we already know—that God is the creator of all beings. This passage does not indicate that human beings are "knit" in their mothers' wombs while all other species are not. It is a poetic way of saying how much God loves us. A metaphorical interpretation is further supported by the phrase "I was woven together in the depths of the earth" It is inconsistent, pro-choicers argue, for pro-lifers to interpret the phrase "in my mother's womb" literally and the phrase "in the depths of the earth" metaphorically.

Proponents of both sides of this issue utilize Scripture to support their positions, making it difficult for the church as a whole to come to agreement.

CHURCH TRADITION AND ABORTION

Looking to church tradition won't be especially helpful either. As with other sex-related issues, the church has not been consistent on its views toward abortion. Abortion was initially condemned by church leaders, often lumped in with other crimes, such as killing infants after birth or taboos, such as using birth control. Critics of abortion based their arguments on parental responsibility (property rights), the "lust" that created unwanted pregnancies (purity), and the prohibition of murder (practice).

In the Middle Ages, many theologians, including the two most influential, St. Augustine and Thomas Aquinas, believed that the soul did not enter the body until a period of time had passed after conception. Abortions that occurred before "ensoulment" or "quickening" were not considered murder and were allowed. Protestants restored the view of life beginning at conception. The Roman Catholic Church did not take its current position until the late 1800s.

AD 160–230

St. Tertullian, church father, said:

> For us [Christians] we may not destroy even the fetus in the womb, while as yet the human being derives blood from other parts of the body for its sustenance. To hinder a birth is merely a speedier man-killing; nor does it matter when you take away a life that is born, or destroy one that is coming to birth. That is a man which is going to be one: you have the fruit already in the seed. (*Apology* 9:6)

> They [John and Jesus] were both alive while still in the womb. Elizabeth rejoiced as the infant leaped in her womb; Mary glorifies the Lord because Christ within inspired her. Each mother recognizes her child and is known by her child who is alive, being not merely souls but also spirits. (De Anima 26:4)

ca. AD 170–236

St. Hippolytus said:

> Reputed believers began to resort to drugs for producing
> Sterility and to gird themselves round, so as to expel what was
> conceived on account of their not wanting to have a child either
> by a slave or by any paltry fellow, for the sake of their family and
> excessive wealth. Behold, into how great impiety that lawless one
> has proceeded, by inculcating adultery and murder at the same
> time. (*Refutation of All Heresies* 9:7)

AD 215

Clement of Alexandria wrote:

> Our whole life can go on in observation of the laws of
> nature, if we gain dominion over our desires from the beginning
> and if we do not kill, by various means of a perverse art, the
> human offspring, born according to the designs of divine provi-
> dence; for these women who, in order to hide their immorality,
> use abortive drugs which expel the child completely dead, abort
> at the same time their own human feelings. (*Paidagogos* 2)

ca. AD 330–379

St. Basil the Great declared:

> She who has deliberately destroyed a fetus has to pay the
> penalty of murder . . . here it is not only the child to be born that

is vindicated, but also the woman herself who made an attempt against her own life, because usually the women die in such attempts. Furthermore, added to this is the destruction of the child, another murder . . . Moreover, those, too, who give drugs causing abortion are deliberate murderers themselves, as well as those receiving the poison which kills the fetus. (*Letter* 188:2)

AD 340–407

St. John Chrysostom taught:

Why sow where the ground makes it its care to destroy the fruit? Where there are many efforts at abortion? Where there is murder before the birth? For you do not even let the harlot remain a mere harlot, but make her a murderer also. You see how drunkenness leads to whoredom, whoredom to adultery, adultery to murder; or rather something even worse than murder. For I have no real name to give it, since it does not destroy the thing born but prevents its being born. Why then do you abuse the gift of God and fight with His laws, and follow after what is a curse as if a blessing, and make the place of procreation a chamber for murder, and arm the woman that was given for childbearing unto slaughter? (*Homily 24 on Romans*)

AD 342–420

St. Jerome penned:

They drink potions to ensure sterility and are guilty of murdering a human being not yet conceived. Some, when they learn that they are with child through sin, practice abortion by the use of drugs. Frequently they die themselves and are brought before the rulers of the lower world guilty of three crimes: suicide, adultery against Christ, and murder of an unborn child. (*Letter* 22:13)

A different perspective was extensively developed by St. Augustine (AD 354–430), who advocated Aristotle's view of humanity in the church. According to Aristotle, the fetus had vegetative life at conception. In a few days, the fetus's vegetable nature was replaced with an animal one. It took about forty days for a male fetus to attain a human, rational soul and eighty for the female fetus. Augustine's dualistic thinking gave him basis for differentiating between body and soul. He wrote, "A human soul cannot live in an unformed body." He advocated the idea of "delayed ensoulment," indicating abortion early in pregnancy was not murder.

A document entitled *The Apostolic Constitutions* that was written around AD 380 echoed this distinction. Abortion was allowed if done prior to the fetus taking on human shape. Once "shaped," the body could contain a soul. It reads, "Thou shalt not slay the child by causing abortion, nor kill that which is begotten. For everything that is shaped, and has received a soul from God, if slain, it shall be avenged, as being unjustly destroyed" (7:3).

As the purpose of marriage was narrowed to procreation, the church issued a number of proclamations prohibiting any action that would keep a married woman from getting pregnant. Many, myself included, see a difference between "pregnancy prevention," measures that prevent an egg from being fertilized, and "birth prevention," measures that prevent a fertilized egg from maturing and being born.

The Roman Catholic Church has not historically made this distinction, nor does it today. If you adhere to current Catholic teaching, not only is abortion wrong, but so is the use of any practice that prevents married couples from conceiving. Among the prohibited behaviors you will find *coitus interruptus* (withdrawal of the penis before ejaculating) or sterilizing oneself through a variety of means. Sins were graded throughout the history of the church according to their severity. Subsequent penance was given in line with the severity of the sin. In the AD 700s the founder of the church in England outlined sins and penance. The penance for oral sex lasted between seven years and a lifetime. In contrast, penance for abortion lasted only 120 days.

Extending St. Augustine's ideas into the thirteenth century, Pope Innocent III also made the distinction between potential life and a life that was fully ensouled. The first time a pregnant woman felt the fetus move indicated "quickening," the moment the soul entered the body. Roughly speaking, quickening was believed to occur somewhere between forty and eighty days after conception—in our terminology, sometime in the first trimester. The pope practiced what he preached in 1215 by ruling that a certain Carthusian monk was not guilty of homicide when he arranged for his lover to have an abortion. He based this ruling on the fact that the fetus had yet to become animated.

> The penance for oral sex lasted between seven years and a lifetime. In contrast, penance for abortion lasted only 120 days.

St. Thomas Aquinas (1225–1274) supported the idea that murder applied only to an animated fetus. His views were respected until 1588 when Pope Sixtus V declared that an abortion at any stage of pregnancy was worthy of excommunication and death. This ruling was overturned in 1591 when Pope Gregory XIV reinstated the "quickening" test. He extended the time frame for ensoulment into the second trimester when he judged its occurrence on the 116th day of pregnancy.

In 1869, Pope Pius IX removed any distinction between a quickened or unquickened fetus. The church now refers to the unborn in any stage as a "fetus." The consequence for abortion at any stage, even if needed to save the life of the mother, in the Catholic church today is excommunication.

→ **When Is Abortion Okay to a Pro-Life Supporter?**

Not everyone agrees, of course, but usually an abortion can be performed if it is certain that the mother will die without the procedure. The two most common occurrences are (1) when a pregnant woman is diagnosed with uterine cancer and the treatment called for is a hysterectomy and (2) when the embryo has implanted in the fallopian tubes, a location that cannot sustain the pregnancy. Removing the fallopian tube will save the mother's life. There is nothing that can be done to save the fetus regardless of action taken.

WHEN DOES HUMAN LIFE BEGIN?

To determine whether or not abortion is murder, one must first answer the question, when does human life begin? The answer to this question varies radically, falling anywhere along the continuum from conception to after birth—

when a baby takes its first breath. A term by those who do not believe that human life begins at conception is "potential person." Those who use this term often imply that a potential person does not carry with it the rights of a fully acknowledged human being. It is thought that aborting a potential person is not on par with aborting an actual person and cannot be equated with murder.

Pro-life or pro-choice activists disagree on a lot of things, but most (if not all) do not want to be in the position of taking the life of a human being. Most of us define the taking of human life as an act of murder. Consequently, one's view of abortion usually corresponds with one's idea of when life begins.

- On the one side, we have those who believe that life begins at conception, whether or not the fertilized egg is implanted in the uterine wall. This view would include embryos conceived through in vitro fertilization, a lab procedure that assists infertile couples in having children.
- The next position holds that human life begins when the fetus loses its gills and tail.
- Some point to the ten-week mark when the fetus's face takes on a human-looking form.
- It is believed that at approximately twenty-six weeks, the fetus become self-aware due to brain development. Some look to this time as the beginning of human life.
- Some assert that life begins at the end of the first trimester. Others at the end of the second trimester.
- "Viability" is the benchmark for some, meaning the time when a child can survive outside of the womb. This can occur as early as seven months, although babies born this prematurely may have serious physi-

cal difficulties or fail to survive. Typically, it is believed that an infant can survive if born during the eighth month of pregnancy.

- Advocates of abortions in the last trimester (sometimes referred to as partial-birth abortions) believe that a viable human being begins after birth and full physical separation from the mother.
- Drawing from Jewish tradition, there are some who believe that life begins when a person takes his or her first breath.

So you see how one's position on abortion almost always corresponds to when a person believes life begins. Gee, what a coincidence! Any and all of these positions can be defended and are on a regular basis. No one is convinced of the other's position because, as far as I can see, no one is listening. This is a serious concern of the church, and yet I predict it will grow in its divisive force.

WHO ARE HAVING ABORTIONS AND WHY?

We have plenty of data on what lowers the abortion rate because we know precisely who is having abortions and why. We can expect 2 percent of the female population to have at least one abortion before they reach forty-four years of age. Of the women obtaining abortions in any given year, 52 percent will be younger than twenty-five years old. That means teenagers and college-aged women (a ten-year age span) are slightly more likely to turn to abortion than women ages twenty-six through menopause (a forty-plus-year age span). More than two-thirds of women obtaining abortions are single.

Of the women who opt for abortion, approximately ten to fifteen thousand will have been impregnated due to rape or incest. Rape can occur at any age, but incest is usually the result of abusing an underage girl. Of all the reasons given by women for choosing abortion, the most often cited is that someone they loved and trusted—a boyfriend, husband, mother, or friend—encouraged them to abort. Sometimes a boyfriend will volunteer to pay for the abortion but threaten abandonment if the woman chooses to give birth to the child.

Economics and racial stresses are front and center on this issue. White women are least likely to have abortions, while African-American women are more than three times as likely and Hispanic women two times as likely as white women to have abortions. A breakdown by religion shows that Catholics account for a fourth of the abortions. Protestants are more highly represented with a bit over 40 percent of all abortions. Those who identify themselves as "born again" are less likely, accounting for 13 percent of all abortions.

THE POLITICS OF ABORTION

The current fighting does not achieve the goals of either side. As the argument continues, more abortions occur. Even though politically conservative Christians have taken strong stands against abortion, the actual number of abortions taking place has increased, not decreased, since President George W. Bush took office in 2001. According to Guttmacher Institute studies, abortion rates nationwide had declined 17.4 percent during the 1990s. In the year 2002 alone, fifty-two thousand more abortions occurred in the United States than would have if the rate of decline established under the Clinton administration had continued. Kentucky is reported to have had a 3.2 percent increase in abortions from 2000 to 2003; Michigan's increase was even higher—11.3 percent from 2000 to 2003.[14]

SOME OF MY THOUGHTS (FOR WHAT THEY'RE WORTH)

As far as I can see, at least three beliefs are shared between these two factions in the church. These are

- An individual has the right to self-ownership.
- Murder is a sin.
- The fewer abortions one has, the better.

In spite of these shared ideals, these two groups continue to fight one another: one advocating a woman's right over her body and the other insisting that, once conceived, the unborn has equal rights to the mother and deserves to born.

It's my observation that neither side of this debate is proabortion. Christians who are pro-choice are not out looking for pregnant women they can drag into abortion clinics. To characterize them as such is to create a false enemy. The goal of pro-choice advocates is the protection of a woman's ownership of her body, not the careless destruction of the life of a child. Pro-life advocates are misunderstood as well. They are often presented as control freaks who want to bring womankind back under domination. Maybe some do, but the heart of the movement is to advocate for the unborn and a world that embraces life.

The best way for pro-choicers to empower women and for pro-lifers to protect the unborn is to give women the support they need to deal with the demands of pregnancy so that they will have genuine hope that they and their babies will have meaningful lives. Would these efforts put an end to abortion? Of course not. Neither will outlawing abortion. Or demonstrating for women's rights. Engaging in the argument, as we are presently, isn't going to decrease the number of abortions. We all need to accept that nothing will keep women from choosing to end their pregnancies if they are determined.

But imagine how many abortions could be prevented if the Christians in pro-life and pro-choice camps combined their financial, spiritual, ministerial, creative, and political resources. We would illustrate that our love for Christ transcends our differences. I think it would change this country. More importantly, I think it would change the church.

Chapter 11

Same-Sex Sex: Is Homosexuality an Abomination or an Alternative Lifestyle?

Homosexuality is one of the most debated issues in the church today as all Christians fall somewhere along a continuum of belief. At one end are those who assert that homosexuality is a sin. On the other are churches, parachurches, or individuals who fully accept the gay orientation and lifestyle. Quite a few are somewhere in between with members debating over whether or not to change formal statements on the subject, to marry gay and lesbian couples in the church, or to ordain homosexuals as clergy.

A SAMPLING OF DENOMINATIONS THAT OPPOSE HOMOSEXUALITY

Denominational statements vary in language and emphasis, although the bottom line is the same: homosexual individuals are accepted, but homosexual behavior is not. Here are some examples from official Web sites for a variety of denominations and conventions.

American Baptist

We affirm that the practice of homosexuality is incompatible with Christian teaching.[1]

The Church of the Nazarene

The Church of the Nazarene believes that every man or woman should be treated with dignity, grace, and holy love, whatever their sexual orientation. However, we continue to firmly hold the position that the homosexual lifestyle is sinful and is contrary to the Scriptures.

We further wish to reemphasize our call to Nazarenes around the globe to recommit themselves to a life of holiness, characterized by holy love and expressed through the most rigorous and consistent lifestyle of sexual purity. We stand firmly on the belief that the biblical concept of marriage, always between one man and one woman in a committed, lifelong relationship, is the only relationship within which the gift of sexual intimacy is properly expressed.[2]

Southern Baptist Convention

We affirm God's plan for marriage and sexual intimacy—one man, and one woman, for life. Homosexuality is not a "valid alternative lifestyle." The Bible condemns it as sin. It is not, however, unforgivable sin. The same redemption available to all sinners is available to homosexuals. They, too, may become new creations in Christ.[3]

The Homosexual Agenda According to the Assemblies of God

Some people ask, "Why can't Christians live and let live, leaving homosexuals alone?" At one time Christians were silent concerning the evil practice of homosexuals. History shows homosexuality has been around since early times, and as long as it was not openly flaunted, homosexuals were seldom challenged. But today, homosexuals have become aggressive in pushing their agenda. The church has been forced to answer.

Today, families with members who choose a homo-sexual lifestyle sometimes call for social acceptance of the deviant lifestyle. Some churches hearing this cry or impacted by revelations of homosexual clergy within their ranks have responded by advocating a gay-friendly theology of compassion. But lowering God's holy standards to mankind's sinful preferences is an abomination in God's sight. As members of the body of Christ, we must not ignore God's clear admonitions.

The homosexual agenda has already impacted public education, public policy, the military, government, politics, business, entertainment, media, and religion. As inroads have been made into these areas, both the arts and the

> > >

> > >

media have openly promoted acceptance of its sinful behavior. Major companies are now appealing to the homosexual market through sponsorship of homosexual events that influence general public opinion about homosexuality. Such aggressiveness demands that Christians not sit idly by as this morally deficient agenda is pushed.

In the face of a militant homosexual movement that is pressing for legal and social acceptance of homosexuality, the church must keep its focus. First, homosexuals are sinners like everyone and need God's grace, love, and forgiveness. Second, homosexuals can through the miracle of the new birth be set free from the power of sin and live changed moral lives. The church must reach out to all sinners with the love of Christ, no matter what the sin. And we must never let the declining moral climate of our nation pressure us into condoning what God condemns.[4]

Assemblies of God

The Assemblies of God believes strongly that God has declared great displeasure and opposition toward homosexual conduct. However, He yearns to restore and forgive all who come to Him, including homosexuals. Unfortunately, many today mislabel those who speak out against the sin of homosexuality as hate-mongers and prejudiced people seeking to oppress and take away the rights of homosexuals. But these persons view homosexuality from a skewed social perspective devoid of true biblical morality. The Church, however, is called to be faithful to God's Word in all things. For this reason the Assemblies of God opposes homosexuality and the gay lifestyle recognizing such as sin. But we encourage all members to reach out in love to homosexuals extending to them the grace that leads us all to Christ's forgiveness.[5]

The Orthodox Church

The Orthodox Church believes that homosexuality should be treated by religion as a sinful failure . . . In full confidentiality the Orthodox Church cares and provides pastorally for homosexuals in the belief that no sinner who has failed himself and God should be allowed to deteriorate morally and spiritually.[6]

This second grouping of churches that oppose homosexuality also asserts that homosexuality cannot be supported by Scripture, although Scripture is usually interpreted contextually, not literally. These denominations tend to soften their language while maintaining a "biblical" stance on the issue.

United Methodists

Homosexual persons no less than heterosexual persons are individuals of sacred worth. All persons need the ministry and guidance of the church in their struggles for human fulfillment, as well as the spiritual and emotional care of a fellowship that enables reconciling relationships with God, with others, and with self. Although we do not condone the practice of homosexuality and consider this practice incompatible with Christian teaching, we affirm that God's grace is available to all. We implore families and churches not to reject or condemn their lesbian and gay members and friends. We commit ourselves to be in ministry for and with all persons.[7]

Evangelical Lutheran Church in America

The Evangelical Lutheran Church in America has welcomed gay and lesbian people to participate fully in the church since 1991, and affirmed again in 1995. In 2001, the Presiding Bishop Mark Hanson initiated a study related to "blessing of same-gender unions and the rostering of persons in committed gay or lesbian relationships." Heterosexual single adults have been "rostered" as a sign that they participate in celibacy as a spiritual discipline. Single rostered people are "expected to abstain from sexual relationships." Including gays and lesbians in the roster extends the expectation of celibacy to all single members of the church. At the present time, the denomination has no standardized policy regarding same-sex unions. The denomination is engaged in a lengthy study and dialogue to discern whether same-sex couples can be married in or if civil unions will be acknowledged by the church.

DENOMINATIONS THAT ACCEPT HOMOSEXUALITY

On the other end of the spectrum are denominations or congregations that are comprised primarily of heterosexuals, but have opened their doors to gays and lesbians.

United Church of Christ

An example of these churches is found in the article posted on the United Church of Christ Web site, authored by Rev. Mike Schuenemeyer, a minister for Lesbian, Gay, Bisexual, and Transgender Ministries. This ministry includes gay and lesbian as well as bisexual and transgender adults, referred to as LGBT for short. He writes:

Open and Affirming is the way many in the United Church of Christ (UCC) declare their welcome and inclusion of gay, lesbian, bisexual and transgender (LGBT) persons into the full life of the church. The message of love and compassion, justice and peace are at the very core of the life and ministry of Jesus. Open and Affirming (ONA) ministries and resources are rooted in that Gospel message.

. . . In developing the ONA policies and programs, careful consideration has been given to the biblical tradition, but there has not been a literal approach to the interpretation of Scripture. Rather, a critical method of biblical study has been engaged, which takes into account the language, context, culture and other important exegetical methods employed to discern the meanings of the texts and their implications for contemporary life.

. . . The United Church of Christ (UCC) is not organized in a hierarchical way and therefore we are not a doctrinal church. The local church is the basic unit of mission and has the basic freedom to determine its own mission in light of God's call. This means there is much diversity among members, local churches and other settings of the UCC on "Open and Affirming" LGBT concerns. The work of the national setting of the UCC is guided by the significant body of social policies adopted by the General Synod of the United Church of Christ, the representative decision making body of the national setting.[8]

Swaggart Continues to Offend

You might remember evangelist Jimmy Swaggart from the late eighties when he was found with a prostitute in a seedy hotel in Louisiana. This little episode made a major dent in his television ministry—especially in the financial support his once-loyal fans had been mailing in. His tearful, rather unconvincing, on-air confession was televised on February 21, 1988. He laid low for a while but is now back on the air.

On September 12, 2004, Swaggart got himself back in the national spotlight when he told his radio congregation, "I've never seen a man in my life I wanted to marry. And I'm going to be blunt and plain: if one ever looks at me like that, I'm going to kill him and tell God he died."

It took ten days of being bombarded with complaints for Jimmy to apologize for this offensive statement. He saw it nothing more than a stab at humor, explaining that the statement wasn't doctrinally sound anyway. He said, "You can't lie to God—it's ridiculous. If it's an insult, I certainly didn't think it was, but if they are offended, then I certainly offer an apology."

The Christian Church (Disciples of Christ)

The Christian Church (Disciples of Christ) extends its acceptance of gay and lesbian people to include bisexual and transgender as well. In order to minister to these individuals, a special ministry called the GLAD Alliance has been established. Its stated mission is "to be a safe and faithful place for the Lesbian, Gay, Bisexual, Transgender, and Affirming community. Relying on Holy Spirit, we speak truth to power, advocating for inclusivity, diversity, and justice in all manifestations of the Christian Church (Disciples of Christ). Committed to transformation, we offer ourselves through education, witness, and strategic action as a visible presence in solidarity with those marginalized within the Church. We stand boldly within the Church to proclaim and embody the gracious call to ministry for the whole people of God.[9]

GAY AND LESBIAN DENOMINATIONS

Last are denominations that have been organized for the purpose of ministering to gay and lesbian people. The most noted is the United Fellowship of Metropolitan Community Churches (UFMCC) started by Troy Perry, "a former Pentecostal minister and a practicing homosexual." According to the Web site, "The UFMCC has grown from one church with an original congregation of twelve to more than three hundred churches with forty-two thousand members."

Metropolitan Community churches defy the usual "conservative" and "liberal" labels, identifying themselves as being in the "mainstream of Christianity," having been "founded in the interest of offering a church home to all who confess and believe." Their statement of faith is as orthodox as the Nicene Creed. They believe

In one triune God, omnipotent, omnipresent and omniscient, of one substance and of three persons: God—our Parent-Creator; Jesus Christ the only begotten son of God, God in flesh, human; and the Holy Spirit—God as our Sustainer.

That the Bible is the divinely inspired Word of God, showing forth God to every person through the law and the prophets, and finally, completely and ultimately on earth in the being of Jesus Christ.

That Jesus . . . the Christ . . . historically recorded as living some two thousand years before this writing, is God incarnate, of human birth, fully God and fully human, and that by being one with God, Jesus has demonstrated once and forever that all people are likewise Children of God, being spiritually made in God's image.

That the Holy Spirit is God making known God's love and interest to all people. The Holy Spirit is God, available to and working through all who are willing to place their welfare in God's keeping.

Every person is justified by grace to God through faith in Jesus Christ.[10]

The difference between Metropolitan Community congregations and most other conservative or mainline churches is that the church is primarily comprised of gay and lesbian members and clergy. They interpret Scripture contextually and, obviously, come up with very different conclusions than their "homosexuality is sin" counterparts.

SAME-SEX SEX: IS HOMOSEXUALITY AN ABOMINATION OR AN ALTERNATIVE LIFESTYLE?

SO IS HOMOSEXUALITY A SIN OR NOT?

Well, that depends on whom you're asking. There are Christians who hold an orthodox view of Christ who say homosexuality is a sin, and those who say it isn't. In a more moderate position, there are some who believe that, while it is a sin, it is no more so than getting divorced and remarried. If a church accepts remarried people in its pews and clergy, then, they argue, homosexual individuals and couples should be equally welcome.

Homosexuality Is a Sin

First, I'll start with those who assert that homosexuality is a sin. This position has been the predominant one held throughout Christian tradition. Most of the time when Christian individuals, churches, or parachurch organizations assert that "homosexuality is a sin," what they actually mean is that "homosexual behavior is sinful." There are, of course, exceptions—those who believe that homosexual feelings are sinful, whether one acts on them or not. But generally

> ### → Moderates Comingle
>
> I'd be remiss if I didn't mention a growing number of Christians who believe that homosexual behavior is not supported by Scripture, but who have accepted gay and lesbian friends and family members into their lives. These Christians aren't trying to change the gay and lesbian people in their lives; they are simply loving them.

speaking, it is the *lifestyle* that is objected to. A motto has been the "hate the sin, love the sinner" perspective. The person "struggling" with homosexual feelings is differentiated from a person who engages in homosexual behavior.

Debates continue over a number of passages in Scripture that seem to refer to homosexuality. I'm going to focus on six portions of Scripture. If you interpret Scripture literally, then it's pretty much an open-and-shut case. Interpreted literally, at least from the version I'm quoting, the passages speak for themselves (but I'm going to add commentary anyway):

> *So God created human beings in his own image, in the image of God he created them; male and female he created them.* (Gen. 1:27 TNIV)

You may have heard the adage, "God made Adam and Eve, not Adam and Steve." The idea here is that God created two genders that were meant to be in sexual relationship with each other—not two beings of the same gender. From the beginning, God designed human beings to be in heterosexual not homosexual relationships.

 One of the largest ex-gay ministries is Exodus. The following has been taken from their Web site:

Exodus

What is Exodus?

Exodus is a nonprofit, interdenominational Christian organization promoting the message of "Freedom from homosexuality through the power of Jesus Christ."

> > >

Since 1976, Exodus has grown to include over 120 local ministries in the USA and Canada. We are also linked with other Exodus world regions outside of North America, totaling over 150 ministries in 17 countries.

Within both the Christian and secular communities, Exodus has challenged those who respond to homosexuals with ignorance and fear, and those who uphold homosexuality as a valid orientation. These extremes fail to convey the fullness of redemption found in Jesus Christ, a gift which is available to all who commit their life and their sexuality to Him.

What's your "success rate" in changing gays into straights?

What you are really asking is whether there is realistic hope for change for men and women who do not want their sexual orientation to be homosexual. And the answer to that is yes!

In 1 Corinthians 6:9–11, Paul gives a list of all kinds of sinners that will not inherit the kingdom of God, including those that practice homosexuality. But he goes on to say, "and that is what some of you were. But you were washed, you were sanctified, you were justified in the name of the Lord Jesus Christ and by the Spirit of our God." Some Corinthian Christians had formerly been homosexuals, but

> > >

> > >

now were counted among the saints. Now, that's good news indeed!

No one is saying that change is easy. It requires strong motivation, hard work, and perseverance. But we find hundreds of former homosexuals who have found a large degree of change—attaining abstinence from homosexual behaviors, lessening of homosexual temptations, strengthening their sense of masculine or feminine identity, correcting distorted styles of relating with members of the same and opposite gender. Some former homosexuals marry and some don't, but marriage is not the measuring stick; spiritual growth and obedience are.

On the statistical side, careful reviews of research studies on sexual orientation change suggest that real change is indeed possible. Studies suggesting change rates in the range of 30–50 percent are not unusual, although "success rates" vary considerably and the measurement of change is problematic. For details and review of several studies, see http://www.newdirection.ca/a_change.htm.

How does a homosexual person change?

We believe freedom from homosexuality is increasingly experienced as men and women mature through ongoing submission to the lordship of Christ and His Church. This

> > >

202 < < <

> > >

transformation enables him or her to shed the old, sinful identity and in its place learn new ways of relating to self and others. Working through underlying relational and abuse problems is a significant component in this process. Making use of individual and pastoral counseling, support groups, personal Bible study, and a same-sex discipleship group are beneficial.

Can a person be gay and still be a Christian?

That depends on your definitions. Yes, a man or woman certainly might struggle with homosexual temptations and even behavior, yet truly be a Christian. However, if someone pursues homosexual involvement and refuses to acknowledge this as sin, it's valid to humbly question whether their commitment to Christ is genuine.

Some professing Christians tout a "pro-gay theology" which alleges that Scripture has been mistranslated and misinterpreted when it comes to the issue of homosexuality. All prohibitions against homosexual behavior are explained away. Sometimes, same-sex friendships between Bible characters (Jonathan and David; Ruth and Naomi) are said to be model homosexual relationships. This deceptive, seductive, self-justifying theology constitutes Scripture twisting (see 2 Cor. 4:2).[11]

God had told Abraham that he was going to destroy Sodom and Gomorrah, two cities that were especially wicked. Abraham asked God to spare his nephew Lot and his family who lived in Sodom. So God sent two angels to Sodom. Lot invited them to stay in his house. After some resistance, they came in and Lot and his family fed them.

Later that night,

> all the men from every part of the city—both young and old— surrounded the house. They called to Lot, "Where are the men who came to you tonight? Bring them out to us so that we can have sex with them."
>
> Lot went outside to meet them and shut the door behind him and said, "No, my friends. Don't do this wicked thing. Look, I have two daughters who have never slept with a man. Let me bring them out to you, and you can do what you like with them. But don't do anything to these men, for they have come under the protection of my roof." (Gen. 19:4–8)

The men didn't go for that, pointing out that Lot was an outsider and had no right to interfere. They threatened, "We'll treat you worse than them" (v. 9). But the angels pulled Lot back inside the house and locked the door.

To make a long story short, the angels told Lot to get his family out of town because Sodom and the neighboring town, Gomorrah, were going to be destroyed. Lot tried to get the two guys who were engaged to his daughters, but they wouldn't go with them. I wonder how they felt about their father-in-law offering their betrothed to be raped by an angry mob. Regardless, Lot, his wife, and their two daughters fled before "the LORD rained down burning sulfur on Sodom and Gomorrah" (v. 24). They were told not to look back, but Lot's wife did. As a result, she was turned into a pillar of salt.

This passage has been used to claim that homosexuality was the sin for which Sodom and Gomorrah were destroyed. In fact, this is where the term *sodomy,* referring to anal sex, comes from.

> *Do not lie with a man as one lies with a woman; that is detestable. (Lev. 18:22)*
>
> *If a man lies with a man as one lies with a woman, both of them have done what is detestable. They must be put to death; their blood will be on their own heads. (Lev. 20:13)*

Neither of these need commentary if you adhere to a literal interpretation of Scripture.

> *They exchanged the truth of God for a lie, and worshiped and served created things rather than the Creator—who is forever praised. Amen.*
>
> *Because of this, God gave them over to shameful lusts. Even their women exchanged natural relations for unnatural ones. In the same way the men also abandoned natural relations with women and were inflamed with lust for one another. Men committed indecent acts with other men, and received in themselves the due penalty for their perversion. (Rom. 1:25–27)*

Many have tried to speculate what penalty these men received in their own bodies, but the point seems clear to some—homosexual behavior is shameful, unnatural, and indecent.

> *Do you not know that the wicked will not inherit the kingdom*
> *of God? Do not be deceived: Neither the sexually immoral nor*
> *idolaters nor adulterers nor male prostitutes nor homosexual offend-*
> *ers nor thieves nor the greedy nor drunkards nor slanderers nor*
> *swindlers will inherit the kingdom of God.* (1 Cor. 6:9–10)

I've used the New International Version of the Bible throughout this book. This translation leaves no room for doubt when it states "homosexual offenders" will not inherit the kingdom of God.

At this point you may be asking yourself, *How could anyone argue in favor of homosexuality from a scriptural perspective?* I know, I know. But hold on. There are other views that hold true to an orthodox view of Jesus and disagree with a literal interpretation of Scripture. Don't make up your mind just yet.

Homosexuality Is Not a Sin

Those who accept homosexuality assert that Scripture has been misinterpreted and misapplied to homosexuals as defined by our current society. Let's start with the Old Testament Scriptures.

> *So God created human beings in his own image, in the image of*
> *God he created them; male and female he created them.* (Gen. 1:27
> TNIV)

Some people argue that the Genesis accounts of creation are descriptive, not prescriptive. There are quite a few issues related to men, women, and sex that are not addressed here. The absence of a discussion of homosexuality does not prove that only heterosexual relationships were acceptable to God.

The next passage to address is the story of Lot and the destruction of Sodom and Gomorrah. Some point to this story as evidence that God was offended by the homosexuality that was practiced in those cities. But if one is looking for sexual sin as the foremost reason Sodom and Gomorrah were destroyed, homosexuality is not necessarily the obvious choice. For one thing, God had decided to destroy Sodom prior to the men surrounding Lot's house and demanding sexual access to the visitors. But if Sodom's sin was primarily a sexual one, another possible interpretation is that the men who demanded that Lot give over the travelers were guilty of attempted rape. It didn't matter if they had wanted to rape the male travelers or Lot's virginal daughters, these men were intent on violating the sexual boundaries of other people.

Ministries to Homosexuals

Within some of the denominations that do not accept homosexuality, groups of gay and lesbian members have organized support groups and ministries.

Lutheran Lesbian and Gay Ministries

According to its Web site (www.llgm.org), Lutheran Lesbian and Gay Ministries (LLGM) was founded in 1990 and "is a national mission society that supports openly identified sexual minority pastors, seminarians and lay ministers who have been discriminated against because of their sexual orientation. 150 years ago, the mission societies of Europe

> > >

> > >

raised money to send pastors to serve the immigrant population on the American frontier, because the state churches
of Europe refused to do so. Today, Lutheran Lesbian & Gay
Ministries (LLGM) is doing the same for gay and lesbian
pastors, because of the 'refusal' policies of the Evangelical
Lutheran Church in America (ELCA). In the decade and a
half since our founding, LLGM's donors have provided hundreds of thousands of dollars in support to congregations
and ministries who call gay and lesbian pastors."

AXIOS

AXIOS is an organization of Eastern and Near Eastern
Orthodox, Byzantine and Eastern-rite Catholic Gay and
Lesbian lay Christians. The word AXIOS is taken from the
Greek liturgical word which describes a truly worthy and
deserving person. Members of AXIOS are gay or lesbian
people who belong to, or have been educated and reared in,
or converted to the Eastern Christian tradition. It often means
people of Greek, Slavic, Albanian, Semitic, or Armenian heritage.
Though AXIOS is a lay organization, bishops, priests and
other clergy have also become members.

Twenty year ago, AXIOS was founded in Los Angeles, CA
in 1980. Interested gay people in New York established an
east-coast branch founded on the same principles as the

> > >

> > >

Californian group. Chapters also have formed in Colorado; Ohio; Pennsylvania; Chicago, IL; Boston, MA; San Francisco, CA; Detroit, MI; and Las Vegas, NV. We have also had two chapters outside the U.S., in Canada and Australia. While Roman Catholics and Protestants have had recourse to their own varied support groups, Eastern Christians had none until the founding of AXIOS, an organization in which all may participate who come from various Eastern Christian traditions.

Together we can render support and positive reinforcement based on our common situations: being a religious minority in the United States and within that, and above all, a sexual-orientation minority as well. AXIOS was founded in order to address the issue of human sexuality within Eastern Christianity:

→ In order to affirm that gay men and women can live an active life of prayer and witness.

→ For our mutual spiritual strength, stability, and well-being.

→ For our desire to bridge the gulf between the church community and the gay community with love and through dialogue, prayer, service, and education.

→ For the comfort, help, and support of our brothers

> > >

> > >

and sisters and their families in realizing the joys and responsibilities of God's wondrous gift of sexuality.

→ For the protection against stigmatization, repression and acts of intolerance.

→ For the opportunity to serve others in acts of charity and love as individuals and as a group.

→ For the study of our rich and varied heritages and traditions.

→ For a true sense of appreciation for each other and to achieve a spirit of fun and enjoyment in our development.

AXIOS includes within its membership most Eastern Christian Churches. We number predominantly Eastern Orthodox of the Greek and varied Slavic Churches, and their counterparts among Byzantine-rite Catholics. We also include non-Chalcedonian Orthodox Christians as well as their Catholic affiliates.

In general we all pray the same Eastern liturgical rites and follow the Byzantine-rite prayer book. Among the membership of AXIOS, we use English in prayers used in our meetings and accept in ecumenical brother and sister-hood all Eastern Christians.[12]

Another perspective is that the sin of Sodom relates to justice, not sex. It is argued that Jewish scholars did not teach (at least not before the Christians came up with the idea) that sexual sin was the primary problem in Sodom. For example, Ezekiel 16:49 reads: "Now this was the sin of your sister Sodom: She and her daughters were arrogant, overfed and unconcerned; they did not help the poor and needy." Sodom, it is argued, was guilty of showing inhospitality to traveling strangers, worshiping idols, and refusing to help the poor.

> *Do not lie with a man as one lies with a woman; that is detestable.* (Lev. 18:22)

> *If a man lies with a man as one lies with a woman, both of them have done what is detestable. They must be put to death; their blood will be on their own heads.* (Lev. 20:13)

Some ask, "Why are Christians today told to interpret the passages in Leviticus literally while the rest are ignored or interpreted symbolically?" The question seems reasonable. Why aren't these same Christians arguing with the same passion for couples to abstain from having sex when the woman is having her period (Lev. 20:18)? Or for believers to stop eating unclean animals like ham, shrimp, lobster, or other shellfish (Lev. 11:1–12)? Or to force single women who are raped to marry, and never divorce, their rapists (Deut. 22:28–29)?

They continue their argument by observing that today's Christians, conservative or otherwise, don't keep Jewish Law because nothing could be more fundamental to orthodox Christianity than the understanding that we are saved by faith in Christ alone. We are not accountable to Jewish Law. Consequently, homosexuality cannot be condemned by pointing to Jewish Law.

It is further speculated that the reason these two passages are literally interpreted and the rest are not is because they support an antigay bias that preceded any biblical exploration. In much the same way as slave owners in the American South used Scripture to support slavery, pro-gay Christians say Scripture is currently being misapplied to condemn homosexuality.

> *They exchanged the truth of God for a lie, and worshiped and served created things rather than the Creator—who is forever praised. Amen.*
>
> *Because of this, God gave them over to shameful lusts. Even their women exchanged natural relations for unnatural ones. In the same way the men also abandoned natural relations with women and were inflamed with lust for one another. Men committed indecent acts with other men, and received in themselves the due penalty for their perversion.* (Rom. 1:25–27)

One of the primary pro-gay arguments asks the reader to put Paul and his audience back into the first century where hundreds of pagan deities were worshiped throughout the Gentile world. These verses, taken in context with those preceding and following, are meant to be global statements about the Gentile world (that's who "they" are). And, in particular, this passage refers to pagan religious practices involving temple prostitutes and those who performed same-sex religious rituals. The issue at hand was the idolatry and the impersonal nature of the sexual acts, not the acts themselves.

Another interpretation of this passage is to assert that when they were abandoning their "natural" inclinations, it simply meant their sexual orientation. Or, to put it more plainly, it is unnatural for heterosexuals to have homosexual sex, which is what they were doing. But it is not unnatural for homosexuals to participate in the same behavior. What is sinful is what is unnatural, according to this argument.

> *Do you not know that the wicked will not inherit the kingdom*
> *of God? Do not be deceived: Neither the sexually immoral nor*
> *idolaters nor adulterers nor male prostitutes nor homosexual*
> *offenders nor thieves nor the greedy nor drunkards nor slanderers*
> *nor swindlers will inherit the kingdom of God.* (1 Cor. 6:9–10)

Some take issue over specific translations and the use of the term *homosexual* in this verse. It is alleged that the bias translators have against homosexuality influences their translations. The King James Version reads: "Know ye not that the unrighteous shall not inherit the kingdom of God? Be not deceived: neither fornicators, nor idolaters, nor adulterers, nor effeminate, nor abusers of themselves with mankind . . ."

Christians who condone homosexuality often argue that the term *homosexual* was not coined until the 1800s, and our current definition of the word was unknown in the first century when the New Testament was written. While sexual affairs with same-sex partners most surely occurred, people of this time did not identify themselves as "homosexual." They were viewed by society as people who happened to have sex with people of their own gender. Formalized gay and lesbian couples were unheard of. As a consequence, there is no Hebrew or Greek word used in Scripture that is synonymous with *homosexual*. Paul and other New Testament writers could not have been writing against homosexuality as a subculture or lifestyle choice because it simply did not exist in society at the time. And they most certainly could not have condemned monogamous, lifelong committed gay and lesbian relationships, because no one in the first century lived together in this fashion. If this argument holds for you, it really doesn't matter how the preceding passages are interpreted, since they could not refer to homosexuality as we understand it today.

But some do not argue over the wording at all. They agree that Paul refers to same-sex relations in the negative. This passage is therefore put in the category of "no longer culturally relevant." Grouped with those in which Paul supports slavery and admonishes slaves to obey their masters, they would say that this passage reflects Paul's personal opinion, not God's Word. As such, Paul's bias was culturally shaped and therefore irrelevant to our life choices today.

FURTHER DISAGREEMENT

Along with interpreting Scripture to mean contradictory, or at least incompatible, ideals, those who oppose and those who support homosexuality disagree on a number of other related issues.

Those who do not support gay and lesbian behavior tend to believe that

- Homosexual behavior is unnatural and sinful.
- People choose their sexual orientation. This choice is made in adolescence or early adulthood.
- Due to the pliability of sexual orientation, it is dangerous for society to view homosexuality as acceptable. This acceptance encourages young people to experiment sexually. Subsequently, they can embrace the lifestyle by choice, become persuaded that they are gay, and/or become sexually addicted to homosexual behaviors.

Those who do support gays and lesbians assert nearly the opposite:

- Homosexual behavior is not sinful.

- People do not choose their orientation. It is established in early childhood.
- Homosexuality is no danger to society. Accepting gay and lesbian people allows them to be honest about themselves rather than encouraging them to hide who they really are.

SAME-SEX UNIONS

Another hotly contested issue involves the definition of marriage. Today, some are trying to redefine marriage to include same-sex unions. Many argue that marriage can occur only between a man and a woman, claiming that marriage has always been defined in this manner. But we have to admit that this is only partially true—and therefore partially false. An honest look at history shows that marriage has never been a clear-cut issue for those in the Judeo-Christian tradition. The state of holy matrimony has been defined, redefined, and redefined some more. Let me explain . . .

Yes, marriage in the Old Testament was between males and females. But not between one man and one woman. As described in chapter 1, men were allowed to marry as many wives as they could support. They were also allowed to take on concubines, women with whom they had sex and children but who were not full-fledged wives. Wives and concubines were owned by their husbands. When Christians point to the Old Testament to support today's idea of marriage, without demonstrating even a rudimentary understanding of Mosaic Law, they run the risk of opening the door to polygamy and reintroducing concubines into our society. This is an unlikely consequence, to be sure, but a logical and legitimate one if the Law of Moses is applied literally to our situation today.

→ It's Only My Opinion

As I've read a variety of perspectives on this issue, I've seen a passion and a fear that runs through them all. I get the feeling that the surface arguments conceal the real concerns of those debating this issue.

First, it must be acknowledged that there are some true "homophobes" out there—people who reject homosexuality simply because the idea of having intercourse with someone of the same sex freaks them out. If you're straight, there can be something "yucky" about seeing a man kiss a man or a woman kiss a woman. And if a straight person lets his or her mind imagine what might be next, that individual can be turned off to the "idea" of homosexuality. I have to admit, however, that the idea of my parents having sex doesn't thrill me either.

In addition to the "yucky" factor, I also read between the lines some resentment on the part of Christian heterosexuals who have been told they should be celibate until marriage. I've actually heard Christians say, "I have to be celibate. Why don't they?" The difference is that we won't let "them" get married—ever. We are supposed to be celibate until marriage. We want them to be celibate forever. No falling in love. No one to come home to. No one to build a life with. No warm fuzzies.

> > >

> > >

I've been single all my life. Believe me, celibate forever is something I can imagine. If I'd been told I'd face a life of singleness and celibacy when I was in my twenties, I may have considered killing myself. I'm serious. I wonder how many gay and lesbian young people have actually followed through on this despairing impulse as a response to hearing that there was no way they could ever be gay and right with God simultaneously.

I think the underlying fear of heterosexuals is that, by accepting gays and lesbians, we'll lose our place in the world. We'll lose the Bible as something we can read in a straightforward way and count on what it says. Somehow we'll lose Jesus and the Trinity and our orthodox faith. We'll lose the historic norm of heterosexuality. We'll lose ourselves if we accept "them."

Right now, we straight people know who we are as Christian men and women, and we know what we're "supposed" to do—get married or stay chaste. We have fussed over marriage and divorce and who's in charge and who submits and who does the housework and who sits in front of the TV with the remote. It's been hard enough for us to sort all of this out. And now gay people want to join in and throw the whole social order out of whack.

And on the other side, it appears to me that gay and lesbian

> > >

> > >

churchgoers want to be accepted for who they are. Sure there are some "activists" who are trying to force their ideas on the majority. But all the gay people I know just want to live their lives with a little dignity. Some of us will let gays in. A great many more won't—at least not for now.

As I've researched this issue, I've been surprised at how many Christians hold to an orthodox view of Jesus and also live a gay lifestyle. I had thought that only the "far-out liberals," those who tinker with Scripture and the divinity of Christ, were supportive of homosexuality. I've been taught that it is impossible to be actively gay and to have a personal relationship with God. And yet hundreds if not thousands of gay people claim to be Christians. As for me personally, I will not stand in judgment over other believers' claims to know Christ. Their standing with God is between them and God. And if God's displeased with their actions, I'm sure God's capable of taking that up with them personally.

So where does that leave us as Christians who share the same church? I don't know. We aren't just divided as individuals. Congregations are splitting. Entire denominations are threatening to break into pieces. The division is more frightening to me than the debate itself. My prayer is that we continue to discuss, argue, and struggle with this issue—that straight Christians keep talking (or start talking) to gay and lesbian Christians and vice versa. We'll only resolve this together. No matter what the outcome, dialogue is better than distancing from those with whom we disagree, especially those who scare us and those we might not quite understand.

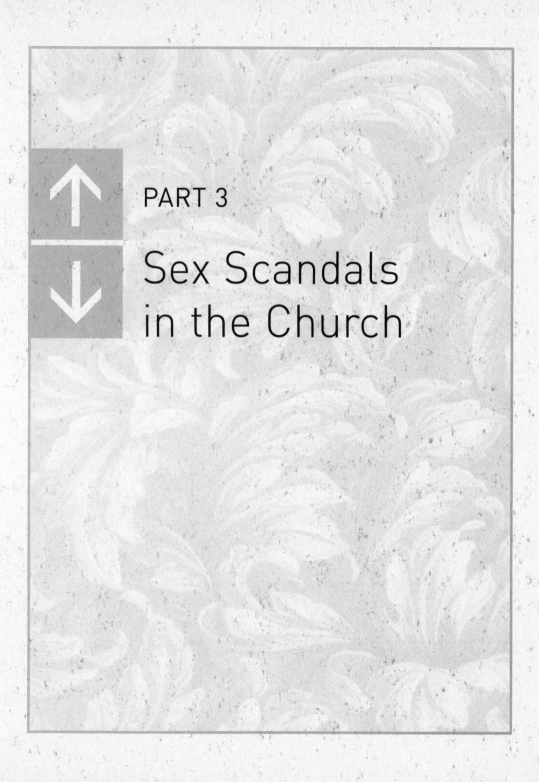

PART 3

Sex Scandals
in the Church

I'll be addressing the issue of sexual abuse quite differently than any of the other topics I've addressed so far. As we've discovered in the course of this discussion, there is definite disagreement regarding what should and should not be considered legitimate sexual activity between two consenting adults. However, when a child or a nonconsenting adult is involved, that is abuse. Abuse is never acceptable.

Chapter 12

Rape

R*ape* is forcing someone to perform a sexual act against his or her will. Usually we think of force as overt violence, such as brandishing a weapon or verbally threatening physical harm or death. But some rapists use the force of their relationship with the victim to disempower him or her. Both strangers and people you know can use fear to force you to do things you do not want to do.

Generally speaking, we group rape into three categories: (1) stranger rape of an adult, (2) nonstranger rape of an adult, and (3) violent sexual molestation of a child. I'll address child sexual abuse in the next chapter. In this chapter I'll focus on forced sexual contact between adults, involving one or more perpetrators. And let me say that I do not believe that women are the only victims of rape. Any adult can be overpowered and forced into sexual contact.

While only women can be violated vaginally, both men and women can be forced into other forms of sexual activity.

> → According to the 2003 National Crime Victimization Survey (Bureau of Justice Statistics, U.S. Department of Justice) 98,850 people reported being victims of rape, attempted rape, or sexual assault in 2003. It is estimated that only around 40 percent of rapes were reported, so we can safely double that number for the actual assaults in 2003. Essentially, every two and a half minutes someone is sexually assaulted in the United States.

RAPE IN THE OLD TESTAMENT

A perusal of the Law of Moses and other Old Testament writings indicates that ancient Israel believed that sex was intended to be enjoyed within the parameters of marriage. Since marriage was defined differently than it is today, it is important to point out that a man could have a number of wives and concubines, allowing him to have sexual relations with many women. He was also responsible for the care of these women and for the children they bore.

Forcing a woman to have sex against her will could result in death, but not always. Rape was largely defined by the location of the sexual act rather than the testimony of the victim. If a man and a betrothed woman (not his own betrothed) had sex inside the city gates, both were to be stoned to death. If the woman had not consented, she was presumed guilty because she did not call out for help. As a consenting partner, she was equally guilty of sexual sin. If, however, the sexual activity occurred outside of town, there was no way to discern whether the woman consented or not—no one could hear if she cried out for help. Giving her the benefit of the doubt, the man would be put to death and the woman would go free.

One of the most difficult laws for me to make sense of details what to do if a man raped a woman who had yet to be betrothed. Deuteronomy 22:28–29 says, "If a man happens to meet a virgin who is not pledged to be married and rapes her and they are discovered, he shall pay her father fifty shekels of silver. He must marry the young woman, for he has violated her. He can never divorce her as long as he lives" (TNIV).

Okay, let's get this straight. A guy rapes a teenager, too young to yet be betrothed. She, then, has to marry her rapist and live with him as long as he's alive.

Of course this is a far cry from how we envision rape and its consequences today. Legally and morally, we hold the rapist fully responsible for violating not her father, but the woman herself. As a society we make every effort to protect the woman from future contact with the rapist. In fact, we protect ourselves as a society by incarcerating him. We certainly don't let him off with a fine, force the victim and perpetrator to marry, and deny them any option for divorce.

Neither the Law nor any Old Testament stories address whether or not it is possible to rape one's own wife. Since women were the property of their husbands, I think it's safe to assume that no such category existed in the ancient Jewish mind. A wife was obligated to have sex with her husband as frequently as he wanted. Her job was to obey, not give her consent.

RAPE AND THE EARLY CHURCH

In the New Testament, marriage was redefined and polygamy was prohibited. Both spouses were instructed to be sexually faithful to their marriage. Violating fidelity was a serious offense. Those yet to be married, male and female, were expected to be virgins. Those who were widowed or divorced were expected to be celibate. These guidelines eliminated "the legitimate option" to have sex with anyone other than one's spouse. Even though slavery was not prohibited, it is not likely that Christian slave owners were given sexual license with their human property. If marital guidelines were followed, children, slaves, and people outside the family would have been protected, at least by church instruction, from sexual violation. The rape of one's wife was, again, not addressed.

Whenever power is concentrated in the hands of the few, with little to no accountability, abuses will occur. In spite of the fact that Christians were expected to be celibate or sexually faithful to their spouses, those who were "owned" (women, children, and slaves) had little recourse in the event that they *were* sexually abused. In a context where a man owned his family members and slaves, promoting the rights of human property was quite difficult. These rights were poorly articulated. I have no doubt that children were molested and wives were raped, as were slaves of both genders—without any ramification to the perpetrator. I have enough experience in this area as a former therapist to believe that women also perpetrated sexual crimes. I believe that women abused their children as well as the family-owned slaves behind the closed doors of their constricted worlds.

RAPE IN THE MIDDLE AGES

It probably comes as no surprise that rape was not high on the list of prosecutable crimes in the Middle Ages. "Boys will be boys" was often the justification for rape, while the victims were often stigmatized—resulting in a loss of social status, often decreasing their chances of marrying. The exception was in the case where the wife of a wealthy aristocrat was victimized. As in ancient Israel, the crime was seen more as an assault against her husband than as a violation of the woman's body and soul.

Along with a growing disdain for all expressions of sexuality, the medieval church cultivated an antiwoman bias. Eventually women were barred from serving as priests. As the church insisted on celibacy among its clergy, women were increasingly viewed as threats to the survival of the church itself. At times seen as vile, seductive creatures, women were often blamed for the sexual actions of their partners. Rape was no different. Theoretically, rape was not condoned by the church. But in practice, little support or protection was given to the women in its charge.

There is some evidence that chastity belts, which I always thought were put on the wives of jealous husbands, may also have been voluntarily worn by women to protect themselves from rape. During the Crusades, when knights and marauders were killing people in the name of God, women were especially vulnerable to rape. A would-be rapist, confronted with a locked metal barrier between him and his goal, may have thought twice before going to the trouble of finding the key. While she may have an increased chance of being physically attacked, she protected herself sexually, which would have saved her from social and religious condemnation. A woman with bruises was a victim; a woman who was raped was fallen.

RAPE IN THE NEW WORLD

Since attorneys, judges, and jurors were mainly white men with property, it was unusual for a white man to be convicted of rape. As white men were less and less frequently convicted of rape, they more frequently viewed themselves as morally superior. The more superior they saw themselves, the less likely they would be to convict a white man of a sexual crime involving an adult woman.

Men of color, however, were regularly convicted. It was much more conceivable to these men that African-Americans, Native Americans, or foreigners were capable of rape than one of their own. "Two-thirds of the men indicted on rape-related charges from 1700 to 1790, and all six of those sentenced to hang, were blacks, Indians, foreigners, or transients."[1]

Viewing black men as sexual predators grew in the minds of Americans through the years. After the Civil War and the ending of slavery, racism took many forms, especially in the South. Black men were lynched by the Ku Klux Klan for raping white women, and even legitimate courts were more likely to convict African-Americans of rape than white defendants.

Women of all racial backgrounds have historically not fared well in rape cases. It wasn't until the latter part of the twentieth century that feminist and domestic violence activists and some branches of the church pulled together for more justice for women who were sexually assaulted. I'm sorry to say that the church as a whole has not been at the forefront of advocating for rape victims. Even though we no longer flog victims of rape as was once done in this country, a rape victim is, at times, still disbelieved, blamed for the assault, or stigmatized long after.

IS IT REALLY RAPE?

We're most convinced of a person's story if physical wounds accompany the claim of rape. This is true for both stranger and nonstranger assailants. If a person can provide evidence of resistance to sexual involvement, rape is much more believable to others. In cases where emotional coercion is the primary weapon of the rapist, survivors of rape have more difficulty in supporting their claims, even in today's more "sensitive" legal system.

Perhaps even more importantly, some survivors of rape may also not see themselves as "victims" if they do not meet a standard of physical assault. Survivors can ask themselves questions such as, "How could I be raped if he didn't have a knife?" "I was so scared I just did what he wanted. Doesn't that make it my fault?" or "Couldn't I have fought harder? Maybe I'm the one to blame." Acknowledging you have been victimized can be terribly difficult. In doing so, you have to admit that for a period of time you were helpless. If you take the blame for what is done to you, you can retain a sense of power, even if that sense is a fantasy.

Survivors can also resist identifying themselves as rape victims if they know the assailant. What if the victim agreed to date this person or was sexually attracted to him? It's easy to wonder if agreeing to spend time with someone is paramount to agreeing to sex. Some survivors don't acknowledge they've been raped, not even to themselves, because they don't want to go through a horrid court scene. Whether charges are legally filed against the assailant or not, it's important to be truthful with yourself and others about what really happened.

How can I help a friend who has been sexually assaulted?

- Listen. Be there. Don't be judgmental.
- Encourage your friend to seriously consider reporting the rape to law enforcement authorities. A counselor can provide the information your friend will need to make this decision.
- Be patient. Remember, it will take your friend some time to deal with the crime.
- Let your friend know that professional help is available through the National Sexual Assault Hotline (1-800-656-HOPE). Encourage him or her to call the hotline, but realize that only your friend can make the decision to get help.

 ## What can I do to reduce my risk of sexual assault?

- Don't leave your beverage unattended or accept a drink from an open container.
- When you go to a party, go with a group of friends. Arrive together, watch out for each other, and leave together.
- Be aware of your surroundings at all times.
- Don't allow yourself to be isolated with someone you don't know or trust.

> > >

- Think about the level of intimacy you want in a relationship, and clearly state your limits.[2]

Perhaps the most difficult situation to discern is if the rapist is married to the victim. Historically, it was inconceivable that a husband could rape his wife. In the 1600s, Sir Matthew Hale, chief justice of England, wrote, "The husband cannot be guilty of a rape committed by himself upon his lawful wife, for by their mutual matrimonial consent and contract, the wife hath given herself in kind unto the husband which she cannot retract." It was not until 1993 that marital rape became a crime in all fifty United States. Some states still grant exemptions, and as I'm writing this, the issue is being debated in different areas of our country.

→ Groups Challenge Rape Law

FLAGSTAFF, Ariz. (Feb. 7)—The 49-year-old woman was awakened around midnight by an assailant who choked her, dragged her by the hair and raped her so many times before the sun came up that she lost count, police say. When she asked if she would live, her attacker allegedly told her: "We'll see."

Usually, rapes like the one described by the woman in

> > >

September would be punishable by up to 14 years in prison in Arizona. But the man accused in the attack was the woman's husband, meaning the crime alleged is considered spousal rape.

The punishment: no more than 1½ years behind bars, and perhaps no prison time at all.

Prosecutors in Coconino County, where the alleged attack occurred, say the disparity is unconstitutional. So in addition to bringing kidnapping and assault charges against the 45-year-old man, they have charged him under the standard rape law, setting the stage for a legal battle over whether Arizona's spousal rape statute violates the Constitution's equal protection guarantees.

"The current statutes are extremely unfair and unconstitutional, and they need to be changed," said David Rozema, chief deputy in the Coconino County Attorney's Office.

Advocates for domestic violence victims say few states treat spousal rape and other forms of rape as disparately as Arizona does.

Arizona law sees spousal rape as the lowest possible felony. The burden of proof is higher than it is in standard rape cases. And it makes no difference under the law whether the spouses are estranged or living apart.

"It treats victims differently solely because of their mari-

> > >

> > >

tal status," said Keli Luther of the Crime Victims Legal Assistance Project in Arizona. "We think this is really archaic."

About half of the states treat spousal rape differently from other types of rape, according to the American Prosecutors Research Institute, the research arm of the National District Attorneys Association.

Some states give women less time to come forward with a claim against a husband, or require proof that force was used. Most non-spousal rape laws require proof only that the assailant lacked consent.

Tennessee says spousal rape should be punished by three to six years in prison, while other rapes carry eight to 12 years. In South Carolina, aggravated spousal rape involving couples living together carries a maximum of 10 years in prison; roughly the same crime committed by someone else can bring 30 years.

Many spousal rape laws were drafted in the 1970s and were considered progressive at the time, because they recognized it was possible to rape a spouse. Historically, wives were considered the property of their husbands, and sex was regarded as a wifely duty.

Luther is representing a rape victim in a separate case challenging Arizona's law in the state Court of Appeals. Also, a bill that would make the punishment for spousal

> > >

> > >

and non-spousal rape the same is before lawmakers this year.

An effort to change the way Arizona treats spousal rape died in the Legislature last year. Some lawmakers have expressed concerns about possible false allegations or the difficulty in proving charges when the defendant and the victim had a prior sexual relationship.

In the Coconino County case, the defendant, who is not being identified by The Associated Press to protect the wife's identity, has pleaded innocent to attacking his wife at a motel where the couple had been living.

Steven Harvey, the defendant's attorney, said he will seek to have the rape charge dismissed because the couple are married. "They can file any charge they want, but it's a charge that has an absolute defense," Harvey said.

Coconino County prosecutors' challenge to the law is unusual. Prosecutors usually lobby legislatures on laws they disagree with, or hit the defendant with additional charges to lengthen the possible prison time.

In this case, they filed a request to prevent the defendant from using the couple's marriage to get the charge thrown out.[3]

Men find it especially difficult to admit they have been raped. Usually the perpetrator is another man, and this can create a great deal of emotional strain for the victim. It's easy for us to assume that men cannot be overpowered, but they can. If a male friend of yours tells you he's been raped, believe him and help him get the help he needs.

It's important to remember that rape is a felony—whether you know the assailant or not. If you said, "No," and he forced you to have sex anyway, you've been sexually violated.

 ## Myths About Male Rape

Myth: Only women can be raped.

Fact: Men can be and are sexually assaulted every day.

Myth: Men who rape other men are gay.

Fact: Rape is not about sexual preference or desire; it is an act of power and control. The motivation of the rapist is to humiliate and brutalize another person. A survey of convicted rapists found that at least half of these men did not care about the sex of their victims; they raped both men and women. Most male rapists are either heterosexual or suffer great confusion about their sexual identity.

Myth: Men who rape other men are psychotic.

Fact: There is no evidence to support this belief. Rape is a reflection of a "macho" society which trains men to strive to dominate and control others and to avoid the open expression and acknowledgment of feelings.

> > >

Myth: Male victims of male rape must be gay.

Fact: Both straight and gay men can be raped; most studies report that at least half (and more often the clear majority) of victims are exclusively heterosexual.

Myth: Rape is something that doesn't happen to "real men."

Fact: Rape is something that can and does happen to an entire spectrum of men, regardless of physical strength or fighting powers. Reported survivors have included a boxer and a man over 6'2" and 200 lbs. Being raped does not mean that the survivor is weak or "a wimp." Anyone can be overpowered or taken by surprise attack.

Myth: Male rape only happens in prison and is due to the lack of sexually available women.

Fact: The rape of men in prisons is a classic example of men using rape as a means of experiencing themselves as powerful and in control. Male rape happens much more often in society at large than we realize, but the victims rarely tell anyone.[4]

What to Do If You've Been Raped

The first thing to do if you've been raped is to get away from the rapist. Go to a safe place immediately. Second, tell someone you trust what happened. Get emotional support from someone who will accompany you through the process of contacting the police and going to the emergency room. Write down what happened so you can remember details.

If you are uncertain about what to do, call a rape hotline or go on-line to one of the many Web sites that give assistance to rape victims. Here's one you can contact: National Sexual Assault Hotline—free, confidential counseling, twenty-four hours a day: 1-800-656-HOPE.

After you find someone to be with you, you'll need to do at least two more things: go to the emergency room and call the police. To preserve any evidence of the attack, do not take a shower, brush your teeth, or change your clothes. Let the doctor know that you were raped so the hospital can collect needed samples. If you suspect you were drugged, tell them so they can take a urine sample. Make sure you ask about sexually transmitted diseases and when it is appropriate to be tested in the future.

When you talk with police, ask to speak with an officer that is your same gender. Depending on the department, this may or may not be possible. Describe to the officer in detail what occurred. And remember: you are not to blame for the assault.

What occurs next will depend on your particular circumstances. Whatever the future holds, make sure you get plenty of support. Check appendix C: "Resources" for places that can help you. Rape impacts you on every level. Get the help you need and give yourself time to be transformed from a victim into a survivor.

Chapter 13

Sexual Abuse
of Children

Any mention of child sexual abuse today immediately conjures up the recent scandals in the Roman Catholic Church. It is a false sense of security, however, for members of other denominations to feel safe from the abuse of children. Christians are no less likely to be victims of child sexual abuse than the general public, and may even be more likely since churches gather together children of all ages for Sunday school, camps, child-care, and other child-related ministries.

For me, child sexual abuse is more than simply a topic of concern, because I am a survivor of child sexual abuse. Not only was I victimized, but the abuse occurred while I was in the care of the church—in the nursery while my parents attended Sunday morning worship services. (We attended a Protestant church, by the way.) When I was around two years old, I was molested by the primary female caregiver. Up until this time, I was happy to play with the other children. But after she traumatized me, I remember crying hysterically when my mother dropped me off in this cruel woman's care. Fortunately for me, my mother noticed my despair and began to stay in the nursery with me, which put an end to the molestation.

But it is unfortunate that it happened at all. I am certain that this abuse shaped my adult life, relationally and sexually, with a negative and long-lasting impact. One of the ways the abuse revealed itself was through my unconscious drive to help other people who have been sexually abused. I became a social worker and specialized in child sexual abuse prevention and treatment. I interviewed pedophiles; I read every book I could get my hands on; I worked with survivors; I taught kids how to protect themselves from abuse. I was driven, but I didn't know why.

The abuse also showed itself in my relationships with men. I am quite certain that this violation of trust has contributed to my remaining single (along with the fact that I'm a handful—can't blame that on anyone else!). It wasn't until my mid-thirties that I was able to "resolve" this issue. I was helped by individual therapy, group support, massage therapy, a lot of prayer, and the love of good friends. No longer do I feel haunted by this event. The church where it took place is near my home, and I drive by it often without thinking of what happened. But who I am now is shaped, in part, by the abuse I suffered when I was a small child.

Many others have suffered in the same way due to sexual abuse. Some experts say that one in four girls and one in six, or even one in five, boys are sexually abused before the age of eighteen. Some experts believe that more than one hundred thousand children are victimized each year. Please note: *Boys can be molested too.* If you haven't been abused, it's almost certain that you know someone who has.

Facts About Child Sexual Abuse

No one knows for sure how often this abuse occurs, but here are some estimates made by experts in the field:

- Most child sexual abuse occurs within a circle of family and friends. Vigilance cannot stop at our own front doors.
- 34 percent of child sexual abuse cases are perpetrated by family members.
- A further 59 percent of cases are perpetrated by people who are known and trusted by the family.
- A significant number of child sexual abuse cases are perpetrated by older or larger children and teenagers.
- People who abuse children look and act just like everyone else. In fact many go out of their way to appear trustworthy to gain access to vulnerable children.
- Those who sexually abuse children often work to create a trusting relationship with the parents of their victim.
- Those who sexually abuse children are drawn to settings where they can gain easy access to children. Sport leagues, faith center groups, clubs, and school groups are popular with abusers for this reason.[1]

WHAT IS CHILD SEXUAL ABUSE?

Each state has its own legal definition of child sexual abuse. These definitions relate to the prosecuting of offenders and can be more restricted than the definition used by mental health professionals, support groups, and others helping victims of child abuse. Just because a situation is not prosecutable does not mean that sexual abuse did not occur. M. Elizabeth Ralston, Ph.D., executive director of Lowcountry Children's Center, Charleston, South Carolina, writes that "sexual abuse or sexual molestation can include any kind of sexual act directed toward a child by an adult or by an older or more powerful child or any sexual act which involves a threat or violence."

These sexual acts include anything from having intercourse with a child, exposing a child to pornography, or talking to the child in a sexual way. An adult does not have to touch a child for sexual abuse to occur. Incest is sexual abuse that occurs between a child and someone in his or her extended family.

WHAT DOES THE OLD TESTAMENT SAY
ABOUT CHILD MOLESTATION?

Incest is discussed at length in Old Testament Law. Even though the rationale was to protect the property rights of the patriarch, sex with family members was unacceptable. We can assume that molesting a child outside of one's family was also unacceptable, as a child of either gender would belong to someone else. The Law of Moses does not include any direct prohibition of having sex with your own children, although I think it's safe to conclude that this was not an accepted practice. In Leviticus 18 we read:

Do not dishonor your father by having sexual relations with your mother . . . Do not have sexual relations with your father's wife; that would dishonor your father . . . Do not dishonor your father's brother by approaching his wife to have sexual relations . . . Do not have sexual relations with your brother's wife; that would dishonor your brother. (vv. 7, 8, 14, 16)

Having sex with one's granddaughter was also forbidden, presumably because the grandfather would violate the property rights of her father. But this law does not indicate the age of the granddaughter. This passage may or may not refer to child molestation.

THE CHURCH'S STAND ON THE SEXUAL ABUSE OF CHILDREN

A direct admonition against sexual activity between adults and children cannot be found in the New Testament. Scholars explain this in different ways. Some believe that the absence of such a declaration exposes the low regard given to children of that time period. Others argue that writers of the New Testament shared an understanding with their readers that such activity was forbidden. They saw no reason to reiterate what was already known. Regardless of the motives one attributes to the omission, I believe it's appropriate to assume that child molestation in any form was not acceptable. Sex, as discussed throughout this book, was seen as appropriate only within the confines of marriage. Prepubescent children were not marriageable.

As the church became more controlling of sexual relations, proclamations were made regarding "marital" incest. In 1215, the Fourth Lateran Council forbade marriage between relatives within four degrees, either by blood or marriage. This included godparents and their godchildren. Incestuous marriages were more common among the nobility as they were more limited in number and more desirous of having their children marry within their own class. These unions could be arranged by gaining permission from the pope.

Overall, the institutionalized church supported the rights of a father over his family, not the rights of children as individuals. By doing so, children have been vulnerable for sexual exploitation, especially within their own families. We have a dismal track record of taking care of our children.

→ ## What All Churches Should Learn from the Roman Catholic Molestation Scandals

It's next to impossible to say how many priests have sexually violated children in their congregations. It is equally impossible to know how many children have been victimized. Some estimates from recent studies and experts say the percentage of priests who have molested children varies from 1 to 7 percent of the priesthood in the United States. Wow.

The Catholic church has not only suffered by the conduct of its priests, but the institution has done what most institutions do: it took care of itself. Seeing itself above the law, the sexual abuse of children was seen as a sin rather

> > >

> > >

than as a crime. If such behavior was confessed by an abusive priest, he would be absolved. If someone in the church accused a priest of molestation, he would most likely be transferred to another area—but not handed over to the police. The scandal has now erupted beyond the church's control, resulting in the payment of millions of dollars to victims and a tragic loss of trust by many Catholics, whether they were abused or not.

The lessons the Catholic church is hopefully learning must not be lost on Protestant and Orthodox churches. Sexual abuse of children is a crime and is to be reported to the authorities—not buried within the confines of a congregation as a collective secret.

WHAT KIND OF PEOPLE MOLEST CHILDREN?

It would be very helpful if we could describe the characteristics of child sexual abuse offenders. Unfortunately, they live among us looking a lot like we do, unless they're caught. Not everyone who gets involved sexually with a child is a pedophile. Some who are sexually involved, usually with an adolescent, may be attracted to the adultlike sexual features of a teenager. This does not change the fact that being sexual with an underage person is a crime. But it's important to note that not all child molesters are motivated by the same issues. Child molesters can be heterosexual, homosexual, or bisexual and come from any racial or economic background.

Types of Sex Offenders

Pedophile: Someone who is sexually excited by pre-pubescent children.

Perpetrator: Someone who has abused more than one child or has abused one particular child for an extended period of time.

Incest Perpetrator: Most often fathers and stepfathers are perpetrators of incest. However, anyone in the extended family, such as mothers, siblings, cousins, uncles, and aunts, can be sexually abusive.

As mentioned earlier, I have interviewed convicted pedophiles. These men weren't selected according to a research method, so my findings serve as more anecdotal than scientific. I was nevertheless alarmed when half of the men I spoke with told me they had purposely gone into professional ministry or had volunteered in Sunday school and youth work to gain sexual access to children. (None of them were Catholic, by the way.) They initiated carefully constructed strategies to fool parents and trick kids. Fortunately, their efforts were ultimately discovered and they were caught. But there are pedophiles among us who are purposely trying to seduce, intimidate, and abuse our children.

Pedophiles are people who are sexually fixated on children. Most of them were molested as children and often target children of the same age they were at their molestation. A variety of treatment approaches have been tried on known pedophiles, none with enormous success. Pedophiles are predators, intent on gaining access to children, and our only long-term solution is to continually separate them from children and teens. And remember, women can be pedophiles as well as men. However, we as a society rarely recognize a female sexual offender when we see her.

WHAT SHOULD I DO IF I WAS MOLESTED?

Secrecy is at the heart of sexual abuse of any kind. The offender convinces the victim to be quiet. If the abuse is discovered, the congregation usually engages in a cover-up. Silence and cover-ups will not result in healing.

If you were abused as a child or suspect you were, it's critical for you to get support for healing. Tell someone you trust about your experience. Do not give up if the first person you tell doesn't understand, will not help you, or is not capable of helping you. Keep telling until you get the help you need.

In appendix C: "Resources," you'll find a lot of places and people who will help you.

WHAT DO I DO IF SOMEONE TELLS ME
HE (OR SHE) IS A VICTIM?

If someone tells you he or she has been or is being sexually abused (whether by clergy or not), do not promise to keep the abuse a "secret." You needn't blab it all over town, either. But you have been selected as someone trustworthy by the victim, and you now have a responsibility to bring to light what was done in secret. Make sure the person who was abused gets the psychological, legal, and spiritual help needed to heal and to bring the perpetrator to justice.

If you are a layperson in church leadership, don't invest your efforts in protecting the reputation of the congregation. Instead, do the right thing and help to empower the victim. Be a part of the *real* church, not merely an institution that is hellbent on self-preservation.

If you (whether clergy or not) have abused or are abusing a child, do the right thing. Confess your behavior to someone who will not promise to keep your secret. If you have molested a child, you have broken the law. You must face the fact that you will most likely be arrested and prosecuted for your crime. It's time to face the truth and do your time.

→ Clergy Abuse of Adult Congregants

While the Catholic church has drawn the most fire for priests involved in child molestation, a great many cases of sexual misconduct by priests involves adult men or women from their congregations. And the statistics from Protestant churches aren't much better. We have had our share of Jim Bakkers and Jimmy Swaggarts, so there's no room for finger pointing.

Abuse of any kind entails a misuse of power. The clergy have spiritual authority, positions of respect, and more clout in religious institutions than do congregants. Sexual misconduct of the clergy takes many forms, including inappropriate sex talk, harassment, various forms of touching, and intercourse. Both men and women can be

> > >

> > >

victims, depending on the orientation and gender of the clergy member. While clergymen represent the largest percentage of offenders, women are also counted among those who violate the sexual boundaries of parishioners.

Some people believe that any sort of romantic relationship between a pastor and congregant is inherently abusive. I don't agree, but in some states, the law is on my opponents' side. I do not believe that a single pastor should be forbidden from dating a parishioner, as long as the relationship is made public. Sexual predators do their best work in secret. Anyone who is willing to be above-board with his or her dating life is less likely to fall into abuse. But there is much debate on this, so, single parishioners, beware.

Those abused by clergy have an additional violation of sacred trust and often find their relationships with God in question. As God's representatives, most clergy are trusted almost without reservation. The betrayal experienced by the victim can be more devastating than the actual sexual activities.

An additional consequence for the victim is alienation from the spiritual community. Since abuse is a secretive affair, a man or woman who gets involved sexually with a pastor tends to keep quiet about the activity or relationship.

> > >

> > >

If the sexual involvement becomes public, it is common for the congregation to divide between those who support the pastor and those who support the victim. The healing of those who have been sexually misused may be thwarted by controversy and public shame.

The bottom line in sexual abuse is to tell the truth—it doesn't matter if you're the victim, the offender, or a confidant. Tell the truth, and keep telling it. Give God a chance to bring good out of the damage caused by sexual abuse. Tell the truth.

Chapter 14

Sexual Addiction

As a society, and even within the church, we toss around the term *addiction* rather carelessly. Anyone who is a bit compulsive might garner the label. But addiction is a serious condition that if left unaddressed will slowly destroy the life of the addict and his or her loved ones.

A sex addict is someone who engages in one or more unwanted sexual behaviors in a compulsive and progressively destructive pattern. A person can become addicted to any sexual activity. One does not have to engage in unusual sexual practices to be an addict, although some addicts have some rather unconventional obsessions. The activity isn't the problem—the compulsion to engage in the activity is. Addicts feel out of control: their daily lives disrupted, their marriages are put in jeopardy as are their standings in church and community life.

A key element of sexual addiction is secrecy. Since most people are modest about their sex lives, it can be hard to discern what is dangerously secretive and what is simply private. For example, I don't want to know what practices my married friends prefer in the bedroom. That is private. A secret in contrast would be if one of my married friends had sex outside his or her marriage. Finding out something private about another person can be embarrassing. Finding out a secret can be devastating.

Sexual addictions often lead to the creation of a secret life—hours spent secretly viewing on-line pornography, a series of one-night stands with strangers, an increasing desire to have sex in dangerous or public places, building a sexual life with one person while creating an emotional home with your spouse—the list is endless. An addict may begin with one obsessive behavior, such as masturbation, and then move on to porn or elicit relationships. Along with feeling out of control, most addicts are plagued with shame and guilt. Many promise themselves they will "not do it again," only to find themselves unable to resist the next temptation.

 ## Characteristics of Sex Addiction

1. Do you keep your sexual or romantic activities secret from those important to you? Do you lead a double life?
2. Have your needs driven you to have sex in places or situations or with people you would not normally choose?
3. Do you find yourself looking for sexually arousing articles or scenes in newspapers, magazines, or other media?

> > >

4. Do you find that romantic or sexual fantasies interfere with your relationships or are preventing you from facing problems?

5. Do you frequently want to get away from a sex partner after having sex? Do you frequently feel remorse, shame, or guilt after a sexual encounter?

6. Do you feel shame about your body or your sexuality, such that you avoid touching your body or engaging in sexual relationships? Do you fear that you have no sexual feelings, that you are asexual?

7. Does each new relationship continue to have the same destructive patterns which prompted you to leave the last relationship?

8. Is it taking more variety and frequency of sexual and romantic activities than previously to bring the same levels of excitement and relief?

9. Have you ever been arrested or are you in danger of being arrested because of your practices of voyeurism, exhibitionism, prostitution, sex with minors, indecent phone calls, etc.?

10. Does your pursuit of sex or romantic relationships interfere with your spiritual beliefs or development?

11. Do your sexual activities include the risk, threat, or reality of disease, pregnancy, coercion, or violence?

> > >

> > >

12. Has your sexual or romantic behavior ever left you feeling hopeless, alienated from others, or suicidal?[1]

LOVE ADDICTION

Everything around us promotes an unrealistic reliance on romantic relationships. In our secular society, romantic love has replaced a recognized need for God as a source of meaning, strength, and identity. Sexual activity does not have to be a part of love addiction, although they often are related. Many of us have become obsessed with finding Mr. or Miss Right, until we find ourselves feeling out of control, depressed, and powerless. Remember, loving someone is normal. Stalking him or her is not.

To discern whether or not you're a love addict, apply the same criteria you would about any other addiction. If your focus on one or more love interests becomes increasingly strong and obsessive, you may be a love addict. If you feel lost or meaningless without this person, you may qualify. Perhaps most importantly, consider how much "danger" you are putting yourself in for this person. Are you attracted to people who tend to be addicted to sex, drugs, or alcohol? Are they violent or emotionally abusive? Is your behavior becoming more and more self-destructive? Are you driving by their house incessantly, wanting to know where they are? Showing up at their workplace and making a nuisance of yourself? If you have a restraining order against you, I think it's safe to say you're addicted. And you need help.

PORNOGRAPHY

Pornography has been around since humanity could draw or tell a juicy tale . . . in other words, from the beginning. Erotic pictures have been unearthed from all ancient cultures on walls, jewelry, and even tableware. Since the invention of the printing press, the production of printed pornography has flourished, as is true of other technological advances, such as photography, filmmaking, videotaping, and various other forms of recording devices.

Before the widespread use of the Internet, a pornography addict had to take the chance of discovery when shopping at an adult bookstore or ordering from mail-order sources. But now pornography is as far away as your home computer and the click of a mouse. Some who would never enter an adult bookstore are quite easily tempted by the easy access to porn on-line. Not only can one view porn at home or at the office, but videotapes and other sexual materials can be ordered on-line with minimal threat of exposure. As a consequence, many more people are addicted to pornography than ever before.

According to Gary Brooks, Ph.D., in *The Centerfold Syndrome,* there are at least five negative consequences to pornography addiction.

1. **Voyeurism:** Men become obsessed with looking at women rather than interacting with them as real people.
2. **Objectification:** This attitude views women mostly as objects to be rated on the basis of their body parts, as opposed to their mind, their personality, their spirituality, or any other quality.
3. **Validation:** Many men develop an almost driven need to have their masculinity affirmed by women, especially attractive women.

4. **Trophyism:** Women become the property of the man as a symbol of accomplishment and manliness. Their worth is based on the increased prestige they bring to the man.

5. **Fear of True Intimacy:** By channeling their energy and attention into the false intimacy of pornography, men never gain the skills necessary to develop deep, honest relationships with real women. This traps men in a world of loneliness and fear of closeness.[2]

Not Everyone Is a Sex Addict

We run the risk of seeing ourselves as sex addicts if we confuse destructive obsession with a normal, albeit strong, sex drive. This is especially true for adolescent boys who seem swept off their feet by their natural physical development. Just because you think of sex a lot does not mean you are an addict. Take an honest look at your actions. Are you being sexually appropriate for the situation? If someone found out about your activities, would you simply be embarrassed or would you find your world turned upside down? If you have any questions, talk to someone you trust who will keep your conversation confidential. Avoid talking to people who are rigidly judgmental. Select someone who is educated on the topic as well as spiritually mature. You can also check out the resource section of this book.

WHEN YOU NEED HELP

For all sexual addictions, getting help is critical. By asking for help, you end the secrecy and take the first step to recovery. If you or someone living in your home is addicted to pornography, there are three Web sites that might help you in a practical way by filtering out Internet porn. These are www.getnet-wise.org, www.filterreview.com (sponsored by The National Coalition for the Protection of Children and Families), and www.Covenanteyes.com.

Look in the resource section of this book for a number of books, Web sites, and ministries for sex addiction. You're not alone. There are people who understand and can help.

Conclusion

This book is the second of a series of Unauthorized Guides. The first was *The Unauthorized Guide to Choosing a Church*. Prior to writing that book, I was not unaware that the church was comprised of many denominations. But it wasn't until I thoroughly researched the topic that I realized just how divided Christendom has become.

The divisiveness among us saddens me. We all serve the same God who is expressed through the same Jesus, yet we've splintered into hundreds of separate factions. The distinctions among these groups are further highlighted when addressing issues of sexuality. Sex is a charged topic to begin with. Trying to get Christians to discuss the subject—I mean *really* discuss it—is very difficult.

A starting point for our discussion is recognizing that sexuality has not been consistently defined throughout the history of our Judeo-Christian tradition. Granted, there are principles that are consistent throughout Scripture, but we no longer own slaves, men no longer own their wives, and we no longer stone people for committing adultery. As we apply these principles to our lives today, it would serve the church well to do so with a much larger portion of humility. Many Christian institutions have been humbled by sex scandals. As it is said, you can either be humble or be humbled. I hope this book adds to and helps expand the discussion among Christians.

As one Christian to another, I offer the information in this book to you as you find your way in the world as a spiritual and sexual being. Unwarranted shame and guilt have been showered upon Christians about normal sexual feelings. At the same time, the church has tolerated the most heinous of sexual crimes to be committed among its own members. Sorting out what is appropriate and inappropriate sexual behavior is not an easy task. At least, it's not one the church has accomplished yet.

Perhaps the most important contribution you will receive from this book is in the appendices. There you will find many resources that can help you as you continue your walk in God's Spirit. It is through relationship, not insight, that we become more authentic and more like Christ at the same time.

My final thought betrays one of my biases—that Christians should begin and end all discussions in the person of Christ. If we base our sexuality, or any other part of our lives, on man-made tapestries of hand-selected Bible verses, the cloth will tear and we will fall. But if we struggle with the mystery of Christ—a flesh-and-blood man who was confronted with life exactly as we are and yet never sinned—we will find ourselves on solid ground.

Appendices

Appendix A

Deciding How to Decide

Jesus and sex—where shall we begin?

Well, one place to start deciding what you believe about Jesus and sex is first to decide *how* you will decide what you believe about Jesus and sex. Eh?

One of the reasons there is so much disagreement among Christians about this topic is that different groups, and certainly specific individuals, are swayed by different authorities and criteria. What may be a persuasive argument to one believer may seem like folly to the next. Do you know what kinds of experience, information, and authorities are credible for you and what aren't? The more aware you are of what moves you, the more able you'll be to sort through the various positions presented in this book.

Historically, at least three sources of authority have influenced the development of the church and its various branches: personal experience, Scripture, and tradition. In addition, groups with divergent or heretical views also shape Christian thought by challenging convention and motivating clergy and laity to more clearly articulate their beliefs. Your personal views have most likely been shaped by these four influences, but not equally. What you believe will depend upon the degree of importance you place on each and how nonorthodox views creep into your faith.

THE AUTHORITY OF PERSONAL EXPERIENCE

Imagine you live in the first century and a good friend of yours, one whom you trust implicitly, takes you out for coffee and says to you, "You know that Jesus guy I thought was something special?"

You say, "Yeah, you spent a couple of years following him around, didn't you?"

He says, "That's right. And of course you heard that he was killed, right?"

You say, "Sure, the news was all over town. I'm so sorry it turned out that way."

He says, "But wait, that's not the end of the story. He was buried in a tomb here in Jerusalem. A few days later I saw him alive, just as alive as you and I are."

You say, "Oh, stop dreaming! Everyone knows he's dead. You've got to face the fact that you followed the wrong guy and get on with your life."

He says, "No, I'm telling you the absolute truth. I've never lied to you, right?"

You say, "No, I've known you all my life and you've always been truthful with me."

He says, "Okay. I'm telling you that he was resurrected from the dead. I've spoken with him. I've even had dinner with him. He's alive. He says he's the Son of God."

You stop for a moment, trying to take this in. "Wow," you say. "He's really been raised from the dead?"

"Yes," he says, "that's what I'm trying to tell you."

You both sit in silence for a while. Eventually you ask, "So what does that *mean*?"

Much like this hypothetical conversation I've just presented, most of us are Christians because someone we trusted told us they had had a spiritual experience with Christ. We took a chance, opened ourselves up to the possibility, and were transformed by our own encounter. Subsequently, we have called ourselves Christians.

The first Christians had no game plan at the beginning. They had no Christian Scriptures and no Christian tradition. They had heard Jesus teach, watched him die, talked and eaten with him after he was resurrected, and seen him ascend into the sky. Their encounter with Jesus was utterly convincing to them, and they told anyone who would listen. People believed their stories and, in turn, told others who believed.

Even though no one alive today has seen Jesus face-to-face, the essence of Christian faith is encountering Christ in a personal way. Some have prayed to accept Jesus as their Savior and thereafter experience a "personal relationship with God." Others find their encounter with Christ most meaningful when they share the Lord's Supper or Eucharist. Some begin their spiritual journeys by themselves, alone in prayer. Others prefer to be surrounded by other Christians in a worship service or in a sacrament administered by a priest. How we experience Christ can be varied, but the experience of Christ is central to Christianity. Some people put a great deal of stock in their own or other people's personal experiences. Others think that's next to meaningless.

Some Questions to Ask Yourself

- How much do you trust what you have experienced spiritually with Christ?
- How much do you trust what others say they have experienced?
- What about personal experiences that relate to less spiritual matters, such as culture, gender, age, and economics?
- Are you open to listening to people of differing backgrounds and life experiences?
- Can people experience Christ in different ways, or is there one specific path all must follow?
- What do you do if someone tells you God told him or her something that seems to contradict your personal experience?

The more aware you are of how much personal experience impacts your beliefs, the better you'll be able to weigh the possible options regarding Christian sexuality.

THE AUTHORITY OF SCRIPTURE

The people who initially believed in Jesus put their lives and their families' lives on the line. Many suffered horrible persecution and death. Making sure they were living and dying for the real deal was of highest significance to early believers, as it would be for us if we were in the same situation today.

Those who knew Jesus personally were the most authoritative in the early years. Jesus handpicked twelve men whom he called *disciples*. After Judas betrayed Jesus and committed suicide, the group selected Matthias to take Judas's place. In addition to the disciples, one "outsider" was given the authoritative title of apostle—his name was Paul.

Paul was a devout Jew who had been deeply offended by the teachings of Christ. He was instrumental in one of the first acts of martyrdom, that of Stephen, who was stoned to death for his faith. But after Paul had a distinctive conversion experience and illustrated his devotion to the faithful, Paul was not only accepted as a fellow believer, but also as an apostle. All but Paul knew Jesus personally, and Paul claimed to have met Jesus in a supernatural way on the road to Damascus. It was a small, exclusive, and authoritative group.

As the apostles and others who had known Jesus personally began to die, by persecution or by aging, people realized that oral tradition was insufficient. The letters and historical accounts addressed to early congregations were collected, along with some other writings that we no longer view as authoritative. Eventually, many writings were whittled down to the twenty-seven books we now consider to be our Christian Scriptures—the New Testament. These books, it is generally believed, were written by the apostles or their surrogates, although the authorship of some is still a matter of scholastic debate.

Not all Christian traditions approach Scripture from the same vantage point. I've observed at least three broad approaches one can have to interpreting Scripture: literally, contextually, and symbolically. All three of these approaches assume that the Holy Spirit is guiding their interpretations. There are strengths and weaknesses of each, and while more conservative thinkers would likely disagree with me, others think Scripture can be approached from any of these three vantage points and retain Christian orthodoxy.

Literal Interpretation

Those who interpret the Bible literally assert that the Holy Spirit inspired, maybe even dictated, every word of the Old and New Testaments to the authors. There is a high respect for the Bible's historical, scientific, and certainly spiritual accuracy. The more conservative or fundamentalist a person is, the more likely a literal approach to Scripture will be used.

 Defenders of the Infallibility of Scripture

John L. Dagg, President, Mercer University

What was spoken and written by inspiration, came with as high authority as if it had proceeded from God without the use of human instrumentality . . . Their peculiarities of thought, feeling, and style had no more effect to prevent what they spoke and wrote from being the word of God, than their peculiarities of voice or of chirography. The question, whether inspiration extended to the very words of revelation, as well as to the thoughts and reasoning, is answered by Paul: "We preach, not in the words which man's wisdom teacheth, but which the Holy Ghost teacheth."[1]

J. M. Frost, Corresponding Secretary, Baptist Sunday School Board

We accept the Scriptures as an all-sufficient and infallible rule of faith and practice, and insist upon the absolute inerrancy and sole authority of the Word of God. We recognize at this point no room for division, either of practice

> > >

or belief, or even sentiment. More and more we must come to feel as the deepest and mightiest power of our conviction that a "thus saith the Lord" is the end of all controversy.[2]

J. B. Tidwell, Chairman, Bible Department, Baylor University, 1910–1946

These writers certainly claimed that what they say is of God. To them the inspiration is not just plenary but verbal. They were not left to choose their words promiscuously. Their individuality was preserved, but the words used were given them of God. Not just the thought came from God, but every word with every inflection. Every verse and line, and even upon the tense of the verb, every number of the noun, and every little particle they regarded as coming from God and demanded in the pain of grave disaster that we should preserve it in its entirety.[3]

Contextual Interpretation

People engaged in contextual interpretation see Scripture as authoritative, while making room for both the human and divine elements. Those who interpret Scripture contextually examine the cultural context and the original intention of the writer, struggling to understand the significance of passages that seem to contain historical inaccuracies or contradictions between different biblical accounts. Scripture is seen as authoritative, providing "all truth necessary to faith and Christian living."

Preachers and teachers who hold a contextual view of Scripture will most often concentrate on one passage of Scripture, exploring the historical context in which it was written, trying to understand the intention of the writer, and attempting to ascertain what God is communicating to us. Similar passages in Scripture, or those that present challenges, may be presented as a secondary theme.

Symbolic Interpretation

Those who approach Scripture as symbolic literature look for major themes in the Bible, such as grace, forgiveness, love, and reconciliation. Factual details are of little or no concern. Instead, the humanity of individual authors is acknowledged as impacting scriptural writings to a higher degree than literal or contextual approaches.

Preachers and teachers who hold to a symbolic interpretation of Scripture often focus on principles that show themselves in Scripture as a whole. Specific passages may be referred to, but such support is not necessary to identify themes in the faith. Perhaps most important to the symbolic interpreter is making the gospel relevant to our current social, political, and spiritual situations.

Some Questions to Ask Yourself

- What approaches to Scripture have been used in the churches you've attended?
- When you read Scripture, do you "believe what you read" and take the passage at face value?

- Do you look into the historical context of the passage or try to understand the intention of the author?
- Do you look for themes and overriding principles?
- If you find one passage that seems to conflict with another, what do you do? Assume that somehow both passages are in agreement, even if you can't immediately figure it out? Look to cultural differences or differences in intention between authors? Not concern yourself with small contradictions since you assume the human authors interjected their own perspectives into their writing?

How you answer these questions will indicate which kind of theological arguments will be more convincing to you, regardless of the content of a particular argument.

THE AUTHORITY OF TRADITION

Following Christ brought with it a number of sex-related questions: Since Jesus was a Jew, did his followers need to convert to Judaism as well? That would mean adult men would be required to be circumcised (ouch). There is no mention in Scripture that Jesus was married. Should Christians refuse to marry or leave their spouses for the faith? Jesus was even reported to have said, "For some are eunuchs because they were born that way; others were made that way by men; and others have renounced marriage because of the kingdom of heaven. The one who can accept this should accept it" (Matt.19:12). Should male believers be castrated for their faith? (There was a lot of concern about men's private parts in those early days.)

→ Castration of Men

When Jesus referred to eunuchs in his discussion about marriage, I suspect a shiver ran through the male portion of his audience. Even though castration wasn't a popular practice among Jews, they would have been aware of the eunuchs from other cultures. Castration has been practiced in India, China, and Africa for centuries. While I doubt that too many volunteered for this procedure, eunuchs were often given a special social status in these cultures because of their unique characteristics.

Castration involves the removal of both testicles, a procedure that can take place either before or after the onset of puberty. Ten percent of the male's testosterone is produced by adrenal glands, so a small amount continues to be produced. However, a 90-percent drop in the male hormone would be expected to have a significant impact on the body. If a boy is castrated prior to puberty, he will enter adulthood with a higher voice, smaller genitals with no pubic hair, smaller build, and little-to-no sex drive. When castration is done after puberty, a man's sex drive will be significantly reduced or even eliminated. However, a man castrated later in life will retain his lowered voice and still be capable of having erections, orgasm, and ejaculation.

> > >

> > >

Here are some examples where eunuchs were created and used in different societies:

Harem Guards: In the Middle East, the guards of harems were castrated to keep them from sexual involvement with another man's wives and concubines.

Castrati: Somebody made a rule that women couldn't sing publicly in the church. So what did they do to make sure someone could hit the high notes? They castrated young boys in the choir. This practice was especially popular in the 1600s and 1700s. The practice was continued, in some degree, into the early 1900s.

As Christianity developed, different Christian traditions answered these and other questions about sex in divergent ways. Even though today there are thousands of congregations and hundreds of Christian denominations, they can generally be divided into three major traditions: Orthodox, Roman Catholic, and Protestant. Each of the three relates to sex in its own unique way.

Originally there was only one tradition—one church—made up of many congregations each with equal standing. Theoretically, congregations in each city were self-ruling, working in cooperation with one another to discern practice and doctrine. In actuality, congregations jockeyed for power and influence, often under the guise of protecting orthodoxy. The congregation in Rome was no exception. Eventually it finagled the title "the first among equals" based on the claim that Peter was the first bishop or pope of the church in Rome.

The trend in Rome was increasingly antisexual, with more and more pressure put on priests to be celibate. The eastern congregations, most notably the church in Constantinople, didn't buy this idea and wouldn't cave in to the decrees of the Catholic popes. They squabbled for nearly a thousand years until AD 1055, when it all came to a crescendo. The bishop of Constantinople and the pope in Rome excommunicated each other. Referred to as "the Great Schism," the Orthodox Church and the Roman Catholic Church went their separate ways.

Today, they each still see themselves as continuations of the original church, charging the other with leaving the true path. Both Roman Catholic and Orthodox churches view their *traditions* as authoritative, followed closely by *Scripture*, with *personal experience* holding a distant third.

The third major tradition was initiated in the mid-1500s when Martin Luther protested against Roman Catholicism. Most people talk about the Reformation in theological terms—Martin Luther saw Scripture as being a higher authority than church tradition, for example. But one of the major motivators for Luther, a Catholic priest when he first took a stand, was sex. He did not like being told he could not marry and also serve as a member of the clergy. Never at a loss for scathing words for the Roman Catholic Church, Luther wrote the following in *To the Christian Nobility of the German Nation*, published in AD 1520:

> And now the see of Rome, out of its own wickedness, has
> come up with the idea of forbidding priests to marry. This it has
> done on orders from the devil, as Paul proclaims in 1 Timothy

4: "Teachers will come with teachings from the devil and forbid people to marry." This has led to a great deal of misery, and was the reason why the Greek Church broke away. I advise that everyone be left free to get married or not to get married.

Today, most Protestant clergy are married. In some denominations, a person isn't allowed to become a senior pastor unless he or she is married. Quite a different stance from the Roman Catholic Church. One Protestant denomination can differ greatly from another. In general, Protestants promote the Scriptures as authoritative, with personal experience and tradition in second and third place.

Some Questions to Ask Yourself

- Do you believe that the Holy Spirit has guided Christians through the years, giving credence to specific traditions?
- Has the organized church ever lost its way and headed off in the wrong direction?
- If a church has a practice or belief that can be traced back to the original church, does that hold weight with you? What if a practice or belief was initiated after the last apostle died?
- Are stands Christians have made during the Middle Ages or the Reformation valid in your mind?
- Do you think the church should hold fast to its traditions and continue to do things as it has in the past, or update its traditions to better speak to the current culture?
- How do you think different translations of the Bible made an impact on how we interpret Scripture?

- When you compare one translation with another, do you find that certain passages may be applied differently?

WHAT IS CREDIBLE TO YOU?

While we are each responsible to God for the choices we make, I am not implying that God's truth is simply a matter of personal preference. Holding true to an orthodox theology sets parameters around what possible options may be available to a believer. The value you place on personal experience, Scripture, and tradition will influence how you respond to the differing opinions presented in this book. I hope these categories are of help to you and that being more aware of what convinces you and what doesn't will help you sort through the preceding chapters more efficiently.

If You're a Pastor in Need of Help with Pornography . . .

Clergy Recovery Network

We mentor ministry professionals all over the world by "meeting" face to face, on-line and on the phone to guide these leaders toward biblical hope, help, and healing.

→ We provide password-protected, confidential on-line support groups to guide pastors and their spouses out of the maze of their secret lives, sin, and deep pain into vibrant spirituality.

> > >

> > >

→ We are constantly developing and posting Web based information and referral resources to guide the most frightened ministry leader toward help at www.clergyrecovery.com.

→ We are creating a network of recovering clergy who can mentor their peers, "comforting them as they have been comforted."

→ We offer counseling referral for ministry professionals who need it. Clergy referral is a difficult and challenging endeavor.

→ We serve as a resource for ministry professional and ministry board questions. Phone and email guidance for ministry professionals worldwide (rural and international ministers use us constantly).

→ We consult with Christian ministries finding themselves in crisis with one of their leaders.

→ We speak at church staff and denomination retreats to prevent the common clergy crises.

→ We are writing to fill the vacuum of quality resources for seriously hurting ministry professionals. Web materials, magazine articles, pamphlets, and book length projects are in progress, including *Courageous Journey*, our guidebook for mentoring clergy in crisis.

What are the five main crises CRN encounters when working with ministry professionals?

> > >

1. Ministry professionals in integrity crises.

2. Ministry professionals in burnout crises.

3. Ministry professionals in a crisis of exposed secrets.

4. Ministry professionals in interpersonal conflict crises.

5. Ministry professionals in a crisis of systemic indifference.[4]

For more information on how the Clergy Recovery Network can help you, please visit their Web site at http://www.clergyrecovery.com.

Appendix B

Staggering Statistics on Sexual Misconduct

- Sex is the number one reason adult Americans use the Internet. One-third of all visits are to sexually oriented Web sites, chat rooms, and news groups.[1]

- Eighty-two percent of adult sex addicts have been sexually abused in childhood. In some families there was no overt incest, but children were sexualized through early exposure to pornography or other stimulating sexual behaviors.[2]

- Of six thousand pastors visiting Rick Warren's Web site, 30 percent admitted to viewing Internet pornography in the last thirty days.[3]

- Sixty-four percent of Christian men struggle with sexual addiction or sexual compulsion including, but not limited to, the use of pornography, compulsive masturbation, or other secret sexual activity.[4]

- Twenty-five percent of married Christian men have had an affair since becoming a Christian. [5]
- Fifteen percent of married Christian men have had inappropriate physical contact with women other than their wives since becoming Christians.[6]
- Nineteen percent of married men have had an emotional affair outside of their marriage since becoming a Christian.[7]
- Thirty percent of married men who consider themselves to be "very religious" (all faiths) have had an extramarital affair. [8]
- *Christianity Today* reported in a 1993 survey of Southern Baptist pastors, 14.1 percent confessed to "sexual behavior inappropriate to a minister."[9]
- In 2000, 33 percent of clergy visited a sexually explicit Web site. [10]
- Of those who have visited porn sites, 53 percent of pastors have done so "a few times" in the past year; 18 percent of pastors say they visit sexually explicit sites between a couple of times a month and more than once a week.[11]
- Of those who have visited porn sites, only 28 percent say their spouses know; 30 percent do not talk to anyone about their behavior.[12]
- Only 4 percent of those visiting porn sites have sought professional help.[13]
- *Leadership* magazine's 1992 survey of pastors showed that 20 percent of the 356 respondents acknowledged having had intercourse or inappropriate sexual contact outside of marriage.[14]
- In a published study of nine thousand on-line users, a direct correlation was found between the amount of time people spent at sexually oriented sites and the psychological problems they were grappling with.[15]
- General Motors, the world's largest company, now sells more graphic sex

films every year than does Larry Flynt, owner of the *Hustler* empire. The 8.7 million Americans who subscribe to DIRECTV, a GM subsidiary, buy nearly $200 million a year in pay-per-view sex films.[16]

- One in six Christian married men use pornography to stimulate themselves to masturbate.[17]
- Ninety-six percent of Christian males under the age of twenty masturbate regularly.[18]
- Sixty-one percent of all Christian married men masturbate regularly.[19]
- "Child pornography was pretty much eradicated in the 1980s," says Kevin Delli-Colli, who runs the U.S. Customs Cyber-Smuggling Center, a unit that combats the import of child-sex photos and films. "With the advent of the Internet, it [proliferation of child pornography] exploded."[20]

Resources

If you have been sexually violated, here are some places you might go for help:

Your Local Christian Community: If you are a member of a church, contact your pastor. A healthy Christian community can be a great source of healing. If, in any way, you are blamed or questioned about the occurrence, get another church.

The National Association for Christian Recovery: I was one of the founders of this organization, so I know about these folks. They really "get" what it takes to recover from any sort of abuse and can connect you with qualified programs, ministries, and therapists who can help you heal (www.nacronline.com).

Counseling: Make sure you find a therapist who is trained and gifted in helping victims of rape and other sexual abuse. Locating a Christian counselor may be best. But it's better to have a qualified therapist who is not a believer than talk to a Christian counselor who doesn't know what he or she is doing. I'd like my plumber to be a Christian, but most of all I want him to be a really good plumber.

Support Groups: I can't overemphasize how important a support group can be to your recovery. Being in a room with others who have gone through similar experiences can be a great source of support, insight, and healing.

Massage and Body Work: I was a practicing massage therapist for more than ten years, and I have worked with many rape survivors. While massage isn't understood well in the church, I have found healing touch to be a tremendous help to people who have been violated physically. If you've been raped, your body is the "scene of the crime" (as my friend Carolyn Braddock would say). Since abusive touch hurt you, healing touch can repair the damage done to you emotionally and spiritually. If you'd like more information on this, please pick up a copy of my book *Is Your Body Trying to Tell You Something?*.

I do not necessarily agree with or support every book or ministry listed here. It is important that you make your own assessment of each group or book.

Books (Listed by Year Published)

Out of the Shadows: Understanding Sexual Addiction by Patrick Carnes, Ph.D.
    (CompCare Publications, 1983).
Forgive and Forget: Healing the Hurts We Don't Deserve by Lewis B. Smedes
    (Harper & Row, 1984).

Back from Betrayal by Jennifer P. Schneider, M.D. (Hazelden, 1988).

Sex, Lies, and Forgiveness: Couples Speaking Out on Healing from Sex Addiction by Jennifer P. Schneider, M.D., and Burt Schneider (Hazelden, 1990).

Victims No Longer: Men Recovering from Incest and Other Sexual Child Abuse by Mike Lew (HarperCollins, 1990).

Addicted to "Love" by Stephen Arterburn (Vine Books/Servant, 1991).

A Journey Toward Wholeness by Don Crossland (Star Song Communications, 1991).

Please Tell! A Child's Story About Sexual Abuse, by Jesse (Hazelden, 1991).

Don't Call It Love: Recovery from Sexual Addiction by Patrick Carnes (reprint Bantam, 1992).

Faithful and True: Sexual Integrity in a Fallen World by Mark Laaser, Ph.D. (Zondervan, 1992).

Beyond Love: A 12 Step Guide for Partners by Douglas Weiss, Ph.D. (Discovery Press, 1995).

An Affair of the Mind: One Woman's Courageous Battle to Salvage Her Family from the Devastation of Pornography by Laurie Hall (Focus on the Family, 1996).

Men's Secret Wars by Pat Means (Revell, 1996).

False Intimacy: Understanding the Struggle of Sexual Addiction by Dr. Harry W. Schaumburg (NavPress, 1997).

Male on Male Rape: The Hidden Toll of Stigma and Shame by Michael Scarce (New York: Insight Books, 1997).

The War Within: Gaining Victory in the Battle for Sexual Purity by Robert Daniels (Crossway Books, 1997).

When Good Men Are Tempted by Bill Perkins (Zondervan, 1997).

Lonely All the Time: Recognizing, Understanding, and Overcoming Sex Addiction, for Addicts and Co-Dependents by Dr. Ralph Earle and Dr. Gregory Crow (Tri-Star, 1998).

Surviving an Affair by Willard F. Harley Jr. and Jennifer Harley Chalmers (Revell, 1998).

Wounded Boys, Heroic Men: A Man's Guide to Recovering from Child Abuse by Daniel Jay Sonkin (Adams Media Corporation, 1998).

Breaking Free: Understanding Sexual Addiction and the Healing Power of Jesus by Russell Willingham (InterVarsity Press, 1999).

Living with Your Husband's Secret Wars by Marsha Means (Revell, 1999).

Pure Desire by Ted Roberts (Regal, 1999).

Every Man's Battle by Stephen Arterburn and Fred Stoeker with Mike Yorkey (WaterBrook Press, 2000).

Open Hearts: Renewing Relationships with Recovery, Romance and Reality by Patrick Carnes, Mark Laaser, and Debra Laaser (Gentle Path Press, 2000). Order at 1-800-955-9853.

Partner's Healing Journey by Marsha Means, 2000. Order from Prodigals International at 1-425-869-6468.

Abused Boys, Wounded Men Workbook with Earnie Larsen (Hazelden, 2001).

Treatment, Ministries, and Support Groups (Listed in Alphabetical Order)

Some of the groups listed here are Christian-based and some are not. I do not vouch for any of them, although I am familiar with many of those listed. I recommend that you check these resources out for yourself before you use their services.

Authentic Relationships International

Gene McConnell, President

1139 Gracewild Ct., Cincinnati, OH 45231

Telephone: (513) 931-1816

E-mail: genemc@eos.net

Celebrate Recovery

John Baker, Director

25422 Trabuco Rd. #105-151, Lake Forest, CA 92630

Telephone (949) 581-0548

Web site: www.celebraterecovery.com

Codependents of Sex Addicts (COSA)

P.O. Box 14537, Minneapolis, MN 55414

Telephone: (763) 537-6904

Web site: www.cosa-recovery.org

Confident Kids

Linda Sibley, CEO

330 Stanton St., Arroyo Grande, CA 93420

Telephone: (805) 473-7945

Fax: (805) 473-7948

Web site: www.confidentkids.com

Del Amo Hospital

Sexual Dependency Program

23700 Camino del Sol, Torrance, CA 90505

Toll Free: (800) 533-5266

Web site: www.delamohospital.com

Desert Stream Ministries

Andy Comiskey, Executive Director

P.O. Box 17635, Anaheim, CA 92817-7635

Telephone: (714) 779-6899

Web site: www.desertstream.org

Exodus International
Exodus North America

Bob Davies, Executive Director

P.O. Box 540119, Orlando, FL 32854

Telephone: (407) 599-6872

Web site: www.exodusintl.org

Faithful and True Ministries

Dr. Mark Laaser, Director

P.O. Box 84, Chanhassen, MN 55317

Telephone: (952) 949-3478

Web site: www.faithfulandtrueministry.com

Heart to Heart Counseling Center

P.O. Box 51055, Colorado Springs, CO 80949

Telephone: (719) 278-3708

Web site: www.sexaddict.com

E-mail: heart2heart@xc.org

Life Enrichment
Wes Roberts
17053 Hastings Ave., Parker, CO 80134
Telephone: (303) 840-4371

L.I.F.E. Ministries
772 Preserve Terrace, Heathrow, FL 32746
Telephone: (866) 408-LIFE
Web site: www.freedomeveryday.org

Link Care Center
Brent Lindquist, Ph.D.
1734 W. Shaw Ave., Fresno, CA 93711
Telephone: (559) 439-5920
Web site: www.linkcare.org

Marble Retreat
Dr. Louis and Melissa McBurney
P.O. Box 176, Carbondale, CO 81623
Telephone: (970) 963-2499, or toll-free (888) 216-2725
Web site: www.marbleretreat.org

The Meadows
1655 N. Tegner St., Wickenburg, AZ 85390
Telephone: 1-800-MEADOWS
Web site: www.themeadows.org

The National Association
for Christian Recovery
P. O. Box 215, Brea, CA 92822-0215
Telephone: (714) 529-6227
Fax: (714) 529-1120
Web site: www.nacronline.com

The National Coalition for the
Protection of Children and Families
800 Compton Rd., Suite 9224, Cincinnati, OH 45231
Telephone: Sue King at (800) 583-2964
Fax: (513) 521-6337
Web site: www.nationalcoalition.org

New Life Ministries
P.O. Box 650500, Dallas, TX 75265-0500
Toll Free: 1-800-NEW-LIFE (800-639-5433)
Telephone: (972) 424-1900
Stephen Arterburn, Founder
Web site: www.newlife.com

Overcomers Outreach
Judy Turnbull, Director
P.O. Box 2208, Oakhurst, CA 93644
Telephone: (800) 310-3001
Web site: www.overcomersoutreach.org

Prodigals Internationals

Pat and Marsha Means

17530 NE Union Hill Rd., Ste. 160, Redmond, WA 98052-3388

Telephone: (425) 869-6468

Web site: www.iProdigals.com

Psychological Counseling Services

7530 East Angus Drive, Scottsdale, AZ 85251

Telephone: (480) 947-5739

Fax: (480) 946-7795

Web site: www.pcsearle.com

E-mail: pcs@pcsearle.com

Pure Life Ministries

Steve Gallagher

P.O. Box 410, Dry Ridge, KY 55317

Telephone: (859) 824-4444, or toll-free at (800) 635-1866

Web site: www.purelifeministries.org

Reinicke Counseling Associates

Aaron J. Reinicke, MFT

2333 Camino de Rios #250, San Diego, CA 92108

Telephone: (619) 298-8722

Web site: www.christiancounseling.cc

Rob Jackson Consulting and
The Institute for Sexual Integrity
6745 Rangewood Drive, Ste. 220, Colorado Springs, CO 80918
Web sites: www.christiancounsel.com and www.sexualintegrity.org
E-mail: rob@christiancounsel.com
S-Anon Family Groups (S-Anon)
P.O. Box 111242, Nashville, TN 37222-1242
Telephone: (615) 833-3152
Web site: www.sanon.org

Sex Addicts Anonymous (SAA)
ISO of SAA, P.O. Box 70949, Houston, TX 77270
Telephone: (713) 869-4902, or toll-free at (800) 477-8191
Web site: www.sexaa.org

Sex and Love Addicts Anonymous (SLAA)
P.O. Box 338, Norwood, MA 02062-0338
Telephone: (781) 255-8825
Web site: www.slaafws.org

Sexaholics Anonymous (SA)
P.O. Box 3565, Brentwood, TN 37024
Telephone: (615) 370-6062
Web site: www.sa.org

Stone Gate Resources

11509 Palmer Divide Road, Larkspur, CO 80118.

Toll-Free: (888) 575-3030 Telephone: (303) 688-5680

Web site: www.stonegateresources.org

Wilson Counseling

Drs. Earl and Sandy Wilson

7501 SE Lillian Ave., Milwaukie, OR 97267

Telephone: (503) 654-8387

E-mail: earl@tsmhome.com

Notes

Introduction

1. Margaret Gill, *Free to Love: Sexuality and Pastoral Care* (Grand Rapids, MI: Zondervan, 1995).

2. Cathy Lynn Grossman, "First of Catholic Scandal Reports Due Tuesday; 18-month Investigation Tracked Measures vs. Abuse in Every Diocese," *USA Today*, 5 January 2004.

3. Rose Marie Bergerin, *Sojourner*, July–August, 2002.

4. The Barna Group, www.barna.org.

5. H. B. London Jr. and Neil B. Wiseman, *Pastors at Risk* (Wheaton, IL: Victor, 1993).

6. Lewis Patsavos, *The Canonical Tradition of the Orthodox Church*, http://www.goarch.org/en/ourfaith/articles/article7071.asp.

Part 1 Introduction

1. For more information see Prolife, http://prolife.liberals.

Chapter 1

1. L. William Countryman, *Dirt, Greed, and Sex* (Philadelphia: Fortress Press, 1988), 151.

Chapter 2

1. Taken from *My Utmost for His Highest* by Oswald Chambers, © 1935 by Dodd Mead & Co., renewed © 1963 by the Oswald Chambers Publications Assn., Ltd. Used by permission of Discovery House Publishers, Box 3566, Grand Rapids, MI 79501. All rights reserved.

Chapter 5

1. St. Jerome in a letter to Eustochium, Epistle 22:20.
2. Uta Ranke-Heinemann and Peter Heinegg trans., *Eunuchs for the Kingdom of Heaven* (New York: Doubleday, 1988), 62.
3. Pope Sirius in letter to Pishopo Anysius in AD 393.
4. St. Jerome in commentary on Ezekiel 18:6.
5. Ranke-Heinemann and Heinegg, *Eunuchs for the Kingdom of Heaven*, 22.
6. D. S. Bailey, *The Man-Woman Relation in Christian Thought* (Church Information Board for the Church of England Moral Welfare Council, 1953).

Chapter 7

1. John D'Emilio and Estelle B. Freedman, *Intimate Matters: A History of Sexuality in America* (New York: Harper and Row, 1988).

2. Ibid.

3. Ibid.

4. Carol Ruth Berkin and Mary Beth Norton, ed. *Women of America: A History* (Boston: Houghton Mifflin, 1979), 134–36.

5. D'Emilio, *Intimate Matters.*

6. John W. Whitehead, "Kinsey and Sex," *The Rutherford Institute* found on http://www.goodnewsetc.com/124OPN2.htm.

Chapter 8

1. Joan H. Timmerman, *The Mardi Gras Syndrome* (New York: Crossroad Publishing Company, 1985).

2. Ranke-Heinemann and Heinegg, *Eunuchs for the Kingdom of Heaven,* 162.

3. Christine E. Gudorf, *Body, Sex, and Pleasure: Reconstructing Christian Sexual Ethics* (Pilgrim Press, 1994).

Chapter 9

1. Lauren F. Winner, *Real Sex,* (Grand Rapids, MI: Brazos Press, a division of Baker Publishing Group, 2005).

Chapter 10

1. For more information see Assemblies of God, www.ag.org.

2. Fr. Thomas Hopko, Orthodox Churches of America, www.oca.org.

3. Statement concerning abortion by Dr. A. L. Barry on 26 April 2005, found on Web site www.lcms.org/pages/internal.asp?NavID=2121.

4. Taken from Salvation Army Web site, www.salvationarmyusa.org.

5. For more information see Southern Baptist Convention Web site www.sbc.net.

6. General Convention, *Journal of the General Convention of the Episcopal Church, Indianapolis, 1994* (New York: General Convention, 1995).

7. For more information see Evangelical Lutheran Church in America web site at www.elca.org.

8. United Church of Christ General Synods VIII, IX, XI, XII, XIII, XVI, XVII, and XVIII from web site www.ucc.org.

9. *The Book of Discipline of the United Methodist Church* (Nashville, TN: United Methodist Publishing, 2000).

10. Taken from Focus on the Family, www.pureintimacy.org, December 2000.

Chapter 11

1. For more information see the American Baptist Web site, www.abc-usa.org.

2. For more information see Board of General Superintendents, www.nazarene.org/news.

3. For more information see Southern Baptist Convention, www.sbc.net.

4. This statement is based upon the Assemblies of God position paper "Homosexualilty" approved by the General Council of the Assemblies of God in 1979.

5. For more information see Assemblies of God, www.ag.org.

6. "Orthodox Statement on Homosexuality," *Word Magazine*, Publication of the Antiochian Orthodox Christian Archdiocese of North America, January 1984.

7. Judicial Council Decision 702. From *The Book of Discipline of The United Methodist Church*–2004. Copyright 2004 by The United Methodist Publishing House, http://www.umc.org/interior.asp?mid=1728/.

8. Rev. Mike Schuenemeyer, *Message Concerning the Open and Affirming, Lesbian, Gay, Bisexual and Transgender Ministries of the United Church of Christ,* http://www.ucc.org/lgbt/.

9. For more information see http://www.gladalliance.org/.

10. For more information see http://mccchurch.org/.

11. Used by permission of Exodus International. PO Box 540119, Orlando, FL 32854. www.exodus-international.org. For more information see *101 FAQ about Homosexuality* by Mike Haley.

12. Information taken from www.axios.net.

Chapter 12

1. Cornelia Hughes Dayton. *Women Before the Bar: Gender, Law, And Society In Connecticut, 1639–1789.* (Chapel Hill: University of North Carolina Press, 1995), 233.

2. From the Rape, Abuse, and Incest National Network's Web site at http://www.rainn.org.

3. "Groups Challenge Spousal Rape Law," © Copyright 7 February 2005. Associated Press. All rights reserved. Distributed by Valeo IP.

4. From www.TheAwarenessCenter.org/malemyths.htm.

Chapter 13

1. From the Web site of Darkness to Light at http://www.darkness2light.org.

Chapter 14

1. Twelve questions to assess whether you may have a problem with sexual addiction taken from http://saa-recovery.org.

2. Gary Brooks, *The Centerfold Syndrome* (Hoboken, NJ: Jossey-Bass, 1995). Reprinted with permission of John Wiley & Sons, Inc.

Appendix A

1. John L. Dagg, *Manual of Theology*, 1857.

2. James T. Draper, *Baptist: Why and Why Not*, 1900.

3. J. B. Tidwell, *Thinking Straight About the Bible, or Is the Bible the Word of God?* 1935.

4. Information taken from www.clergyrecovery.com.

Appendix B

1. Jane E. Brody, "Cybersex Leads to Psychological Disorder," *New York Times*, 22 May 2000.

2. Dr. Patrick Carnes, *Don't Call It Love: Recovery from Sexual Addiction* (New York: Bantam, 1991), 42-44.

3. From a 2002 survey by Rick Warren, pastor of Saddleback Community Church in Mission Viejo, CA. August, 2000. Survey of its readership by *Christianity Today* magazine.

4. Archibald Hart, *The Sexual Man* (Dallas: Word Publishing, 1994).

5. Ibid.

6. Ibid.

7. Ibid.

8. Samuel S. James and Cynthia L. James, *The James Report* (A report of a nine-year survey of eight thousand men.) For more information see http://www.iprodigals.org/stats.htm.

9. Cagney, "Sexual Abuse in Churches Not Limited to Clergy."

10. *Christianity Today*, 5 March 2001, 44–45.

11. Ibid.

12. Ibid.

13. Ibid.

14. "Leadership Family and Ministry Survey Summary," *Christianity Today*, Research Department, July 1992.

On

15. Alison Bass, "Addiction to Cybersex Symptomatic of Other Woes," *The Boston Globe,* 14 June 1999.

16. Timothy Egan. "Erotica, Inc." *New York Times,* October 23, 2000.

17. Dr. Archibald D. Hart. *1994: The Hart Report*; confidential survey of 600 men.

18. Ibid.

19. Ibid.

20. Rod Nordland and Jeffrey Bartholet, "The Web's Dark Secret" *Newsweek,* March 19, 2001, p. 46.

Index